THE
Irreplaceable
MOTHER

Embracing Your Sacred Calling

By

Jodi Dauses

Published by hope*books
2217 Matthews Township Pkwy
Suite D302
Matthews, NC 28105
www.hopebooks.com

hope*books is a division of hope*media network

Printed in the United States of America by hope*books

First paperback edition.
Paperback ISBN: 979-89185-042-2
Hardcover ISBN: 979-8-89185-043-9
Ebook ISBN: 979-8-89185-044-6
Library of Congress Number: 2024931107

Photo Credit: Laura White

All Bible references use The Holy Bible, Revised Standard Version (RSV), Second Catholic Edition. Ignatius Press, San Francisco, unless otherwise stated.

hope*books
hopebooks.com

"In *The Irreplaceable Mother*, Jodi Dauses beautifully captures the essence of motherhood, offering invaluable insights and practical advice for every mom out there. With her heartfelt storytelling and relatable antidotes, Jodi reminds us of the unique power and impact that a mother has on her children's lives. This is a treasure trove of wisdom that will inspire mothers to turn their hearts towards home. An empowering book- a must-read for any mother looking to create a meaningful and fulfilling life for herself and her family."

Lisa Brenninkmeyer, Founder of *Walking With Purpose* and Author

"It's been said that motherhood is the scariest hood you'll ever go through, and as a mom of four and licensed foster mom, I can empathize. Being a mom is hard work, and during my husband's seasons of deployment, my flesh often told me that motherhood wasn't noble while I had a mob of toddlers in my home juggling the challenges of solo parenting. Jodi's message is spot on - that we as moms are irreplaceable and God called us into this role, and He will equip us to carry out our calling. Jodi is a natural encourager and gifted writer who equips her readers with a confidence boost to embrace the sacred calling of being a mom. The world tells us we should embrace pursuits outside the home, but the Biblical perspective shows us that serving our families is a blessed calling. I loved the uplifting and sincere message that Jodi shares with her readers in her book."

Annie Weber, Author of *Astounding Truths of the Bible*

"As the attack on women and the family rages on, I could not imagine a better book to keep on your shelf. With vulnerability, honesty, and humor, Jodi Marie Dauses reaches every mother's heart, pointing us to our purpose and reminding us of the truth the culture wants us to forget: *we are irreplaceable.* Loaded with practical advice, faith, and wisdom, Jodi is the friend and mentor every mama needs!"

Laura Phelps, Author and *Walking With Purpose* Content Creator

This book is dedicated to the woman who devoted her entire beautiful heart to shepherding mine. Mama, thank you for introducing me to Jesus and teaching me to follow Him.

You are irreplaceable.

Table of Contents

*"While you are still alive and have breath in you,
do not let anyone take your place."*
Sirach 33:20

The Inlet

*"Making the decision to have a child - it is momentous. It is to decide
forever to have your heart go walking around outside of your body."*
Elizabeth Stone

The ocean tide off the coast of Myrtle Beach was low that morning.
Ridiculously low. So low that my husband and I, along with our
four young children, abandoned our striped umbrella in front of our
high-rise condo to take a stroll. We haphazardly left our life jackets
in the sand to lazily tip-toe north up the Atlantic coast, loading our
pockets with sea shells. Our youngest toddled along, pointing out
pelicans. Our walk was glorious, the sun warm above the ocean, and
the view was breathtaking.

Our crew of six was on vacation in a tiny sleepy beach town on
the ocean banks of South Carolina. We had come for replenishment
and rest, but the sitting and sunning had left me restless. I had been
laid up for the past eight weeks following a hysterectomy and some
severe complications which required emergency surgery. The recovery
had taken a toll. But the post-surgery fog was finally wearing off, and
I was starting to feel like my old self again. My spontaneous spirit was
kicking back in.

As we dreamily made our way past blocks of high-rise vacation
condos that lined the beach, the air quieted, and tourists disappeared.
And that's when we stumbled upon House Creek. It looked like an
innocent inlet river jutting out from a tiny touristy town. Clear and
calm and seemingly shallow, the water invited us in. Our eyes followed

its long trek east as it twisted right downstream and eventually dumped hundreds of yards away into the Atlantic Ocean. We watched as the calm creek gave way to dangerous, crashing waves as it met the ocean.

Down there, where the creek married the ocean, there was no way our young crew could swim among the thrashing water at all, especially without life jackets. But upstream, where we were standing, the creek looked inviting and refreshing. There was a sandy bank about 50 yards on the other side, and we (the kids and I) thought it would be fun to swim across the water and look for more shells on the other side of the creek. An avid fisherman and boater, my husband cautioned that this type of water is often much more dangerous than it appears on the surface. He understood the vulnerability of hidden currents and tides. How I wish I had taken heed of his wise warning.

Instead, I circled my arms wide and ushered my children and husband into a family huddle. "Let's all wade into the water to cool off!" I said, pointing to the crystal clear South Carolina inlet rushing past our toes. Plus, I was hot, like dripping-with-sweat hot, (and a bit grouchy and secretly wondering if menopause was already descending on my 38-year-old body just months after losing my uterus. Was that possible? I made a mental note to Google that later).

Our oldest two daughters, Lillian and Lacey, didn't hesitate to jump in. Shaking his head, my husband smiled and held onto our six-year-old only son, Tripp, as they waded in behind the girls. Knowing I needed to be careful because my body was still healing, I lingered on the shore with our youngest daughter Annabelle as I sucked down the remaining drops from my styrofoam cup of hot tea I had carried with me during the walk (the hot beverage probably contributing to my near hot-flash). Without permission, our petite three-year-old Annabelle jumped into the shallow water to follow her Daddy. I threw down my white-rimmed cup onto the sandy shore and quickly waded in after her. She giggled fiercely as I reached out and pulled her close.

"Oh no you don't!" I playfully scolded. "Not without an adult and certainly not without a life jacket, little one!" The water felt glorious. It was cool and calm and simply refreshing. The water where we all entered was waist-deep on me. My feet secure on a sandy bank below.

What we didn't realize was that the water dropped off steeply just a few feet away. And that's how fast it happened. Within seconds, we were swimming literally into a nightmare. Our older daughters were attempting to cross the creek to get to the sandy bank on the other side. The invisible current swept them both up at a frightening pace. In less than one minute, my middle daughter was in trouble and rapidly heading downstream at a furious speed. Her body was completely vertical in the water, her blonde head barely above the surface. I was a lifeguard for almost a decade. I knew a vertical swimmer is a troubled swimmer. Not understanding the danger they were in, as they were swept downstream together, our oldest daughter Lilli was laughing and prodding her sister Lacey to swim harder to try and make it to the other shore. But Lacey was heading toward disaster.. I knew it. And Lilli was next.

As I held my youngest, the water lapping my sides, my voice cracked as I begged my husband, D.J., to immediately go after our girls. Sensing the same danger, D.J. asked if I was okay as he handed me our boy. I nodded yes as I watched him swim fast to the middle of the creek and then let the current sweep him up and carry him to our girls. I held my breath, feeling helpless as I looked on. He seemed to reach both of our girls within thirty seconds, although it felt like an eternity. He scooped them up, sternly barking for them to wrap their arms around his strong shoulders. My husband rescued our girls.

As I looked on, I held tightly to our two youngest children as the cool water rushed past my mid-section. Seeing my older girls were safe in the clutches of my husband's arms, I felt my body exhale. Although they were still heading swiftly downstream, my husband was with them. He would never let them go. With his protection, I knew they would make it. My heart was racing at the close call. I felt so foolish that I had even let them get in, especially against my husband's wisdom. I turned my body toward the sandy shore, desperate to get the other two children to safety.

Finally understanding the covert dangers of the water my husband had warned me about, I turned my body clockwise, back upstream, to try to find my way out, but the current pushed violently back. And that's when I lost my footing. Completely unaware of the jeopardy we were in, Annabelle flailed and let go of my grasp. I stepped slightly to the right to grab hold of her, loudly commanding her to hold tight to me. But the sandy bottom, where my feet had stood planted seconds earlier, suddenly vanished. Horrified, I found myself treading water, holding two children above my head. I kicked my feet around, desperately trying to find somewhere to gain some traction. An avid swimmer, the current was the strongest I had ever experienced.

My two younger children and I were now in serious trouble. I was working so hard to stay afloat that I didn't have the energy to yell for help. Come quickly, please, I mentally called out to D.J., but he was with our girls over a football field distance downstream. I whispered in both kids' ears, "If Mama goes underwater, just hold on to my head. Do not let go. Keep your head above water. Just hold on to me."

With every ounce of energy left in me, I treaded water, my eyes scouring the shoreline, looking for help. I saw a family walking far away, down the beach, but they were out of earshot. Help was not coming.

I mentally surveyed my options. I could stop treading water and surrender to the rapid current, letting it rush us downstream. But I knew it would be impossible to keep hold of two children and still keep my head above water. The water was so swift that it would be only seconds before one of the children was submerged. The current was moving so fiercely that D.J. would be unable to reach any of us before we hit the impending breakers if Tripp or Annabelle even made it that far. They were too little to survive on their own.

In that moment, the horrific reality of what was about to happen to one of my children flashed before my eyes. I just knew, with every fiber in my being, that one of my children and possibly two were on the brink of drowning.

I had only seconds of energy left to keep treading with my legs while my arms circled my children. My right side had a shooting pain where my interior sutures were still healing. The effort of keeping two kids above water was exhausting.

"Help me, Jesus. Please help me, Lord. Please save us..." I muttered out loud.

My son started to whimper.

"Jesus. Please help me hold on. Please Jesus..." I felt a stabbing pain radiate down my pelvis. My biceps were burning, and I had a cramp in my left shoulder from holding the kids above my head. Both of my kids started to cry. At this point, I was bobbing my head up and down beneath the surface, pushing their heads above water and trying to stay afloat.

"Hold on to me. Just keep holding on...dear Jesus, please help us!"

D.J. was still trying to make his way out of the water. I was sure he would be too late.

"Holy Spirit, please help me save these children...please Jesus...give me a little more strength to hold on..." And then, in my last breath, I went underwater and held both kids above my head. I knew this was it.

"Surrender them, Jodi. Trust me with my beloved children."

At that moment, I felt my foot hit something. With all I had, I anchored my right foot in the sand beneath, the current still tugging at my other flailing leg. I pushed my head above water, pulled my body toward shore, and then felt for the bottom with the other foot. The river was still wrestling so strong, daring to rip my children from my arms. I kept praying, trying desperately to hold my stance.

"I am here, Jodi. Just hold on."

Both feet planted on the sandy ground, I found myself waist-deep again. But my body was no match for the slick current. I was fighting to stay stationary in rushing water with all I had. We were not safe yet. The slightest shift could cause me to lose my footing again. I could barely breathe.

"Please, Jesus. Just help me hold on for one more minute. Please help me," I whispered. I knew I had to return to where that styrofoam coffee cup was lying on the shore because that was where we had entered the water and the safety of the sand bar. This was our last chance. There was no help. It was now or never.

With one last breath, I pushed closer, pulling us parallel to where that cup lay on the shore, and with the bit of energy I had yet, I hoisted our littlest one up to the dry sand. Annabelle landed roughly on the shore. With pain shooting down into my pelvis, I heaved my son up there next, just as my husband and daughter finally exited the water downstream and came racing to our aid. I pulled my body from the water and plopped down on the hot sand.

Exhausted and overcome with how close we had come to drowning, I was too exhausted to speak. I started silently sobbing. No tears or sound came as my body heaved up and down. I was too weary to even stand.

Hours later, my husband and I were still in shock. We had narrowly escaped a major tragedy by the grace of God. We could have easily lost our middle daughter. We could have easily lost our youngest two children. And there was no way I would've ever lost a child without going down with one of them. For days, I kept reliving the scene. It consumed my dreams every night for the rest of the summer. I hated myself for not heeding my husband's advice. I could not forgive myself for foolishly putting my children's lives in danger. It will haunt me forever.

But something else, something greater, is also lodged in my memory forever. That evening, after our horrific experience with the inlet, I remember standing in the doorway at bedtime, watching my husband and only son kneel at the bedside to pray. When my husband finished with the sign of the cross, I overheard our little guy tell his Daddy, "Today, in the water, Mama, just kept praying. She kept whispering to Jesus." I walked in, sat down next to both, and slid my arms around my boy's shoulders. I breathed him in. My throat caught, remembering how close I had come to losing him just hours earlier. I pushed a lock of bleach blonde hair back from his temple.

"Were you scared, baby? When we were in the water, were you afraid?" My words came out sloppy, with too much emotion to hold back.

He smiled big. "No, mam!"

I wrapped my arms tighter around my boy. Tears stung my eyes.

"Mama?" his blue eyes looking up at me.

"Yes, baby."

My boy touched my face. "I knew we were okay today because you would never let us go. I knew you would protect us. No one else in this whole world would hold on to me as tightly as you. **God gave me you, Mama. No one can replace you.**"

My dear reader, I am certain you need to hear this same truth today. Even amid a mothering misjudgment, God used that harrowing situation to teach me and my children about His unending, abundant, rescuing love. He walks alongside each of us in motherhood as our protective guide. You are irreplaceable. Even when you mess up, make bad decisions, or fall short of being the patient Mama you long to be, you are answering a holy call. You are given a sacred assignment to raise the little souls in your care, and you are a fierce warrior. How do I know? Because God made you a mother. You have been gifted a vocation with eternal consequences. And no one can love, protect, and shepherd your child as well as you. There is no substitute for you.

Do you believe that as a mother, you have an irreplaceable role in your child's life that only you can fill? My dear sister, I am writing to tell you that you do. You have been given the divine calling of shepherding a soul, and you are called by God to mother. Often, in the hectic and overwhelming responsibilities of raising children, we lose sight of what mothering is all about. I pray that this book will reorient and guide you in your mission of motherhood.

MOTHER [muh*th*- *er*] -*noun*

1. One person who does the work of twenty. For free.

(See also: 'masochist,' 'loony,' **'saint,'**)

PART I:

THE PRIVILEGE
EMBRACING YOUR CALLING

PRIVILEGE [priv-uh-lij] *-noun*

1. an unearned honor to do something special or enjoyable.

(See also: 'right,' 'authority,' 'freedom,' 'opportunity')

1

The Calling

"Vocation, more than our own choice, is a response to the Lord's unmerited call." [1]

Pope Francis

I'll never forget the first time when I realized I was replaceable. Because it stung. It hurt like heck.

My television news director, Dawn, tugged at her blue-rimmed reading glasses and rose quickly from her squeaky chair. I glanced around, nervous about what I was about to confess to her and how my decision would radically alter my life. Dawn's desk was piled high with manila assignment files. CNN headline news flashed on the television screen suspended high in the left corner of her dark office, and the police scanner was yapping non-stop. She held a black cell phone in one hand, with a frantic photographer waiting on hold for directions to a breaking story, as she tapped her fingers on her cluttered desk, obviously irritated with me. Her words at my admission came out sharply, "Jodi, don't get me wrong. You are fantastic on-air, but we have dozens of reporters who would jump in a heartbeat to have your anchor chair. You are an asset here, and we appreciate your hard work, but...if you decide to walk away, you can be replaced."

Dawn had taken a big risk in hiring me, and her gamble was paying off. I had arrived at this ABC News-Affiliate, tucked inside of a sleepy town on Maryland's Eastern Shore, young and green. Hungry and desperate to succeed. After begging Dawn for an (unpaid) internship, I was willing to tackle any task, no matter how menial, to learn the business inside and out. Whatever task in the newsroom she threw at me, I did it with a smile. When a photographer called in sick and we had breaking news of a fire ravaging a downtown courthouse building, I grabbed a camera and learned to shoot. When one of our sportscasters was fired, I cut tape for NASCAR races and wrote football reel commentary. When we were short-staffed, I volunteered to cover early morning shifts in the control room. My willingness to do the dirty jobs paid off.

During my senior year of college, Dawn hired me as the new weekend producer and political field reporter. Just months later, I hustled to secure the coveted weekend news anchor chair, immersing myself in all the local political happenings in our market. Dawn made it publicly known to the newsroom, as she promoted me each step of the way, that she was betting I was in this for the long haul. When I took over the weekend anchor chair, our station ratings, once dismal, were slowly climbing. I had a good rapport with our news staff. I made my deadlines and drew accolades for covering LIVE news. And now she wanted me to sign a contract, she needed me to be all in.

So, I knew my recent hesitation about moving forward with my employment was taking my news director by surprise. She didn't have time for me to second guess signing a non-compete contract with the news station. She needed to lock in my commitment for the next two years. I was either all in. . . or I would be replaced. Immediately.

"Have you really thought this through?" Dawn pushed me. "You have worked so hard to get here. You have earned that anchor chair. After all those crazy hours you put in as a producer and a field reporter, are you sure you want to give up this dream job? Why not sign the contract and then give it some more time? I'm sure your reservations about your personal life will pass." As I listened, I bit my lip to keep my eyes from tearing over. Walking away from my dream of being a television news anchor and reporter seemed foolish. But a recent, unexpected encounter with God rattled my heart and redirected my plans. Something unfamiliar and surprising was stirring in my heart.

Just weeks earlier, on one scorching July afternoon, hours before I was to clock in to anchor the evening shift, I was walking alone along the beach of the Atlantic Coast. My husband's large and boisterous extended family had invited us to join their annual vacation getaway. It was conveniently located in the town next to the news station. During the daylight, I would hang out splashing in the water and baking under the hot sun with all of the cousins, and then when afternoon rushed in, I would race to shower, dress, and put on full make-up to cover the evening news, working late into the night. I was at a pivotal point in my blossoming career and adored my job. But things were not going as smoothly in my new marriage at home.

Although my professional life was soaring, the TV hours and stressful newsroom took a toll on my relationship with my husband. I found myself confiding my concern to God. I confessed I felt stuck between following my ambitions and nurturing my marriage. I was frustrated and confused, and I let God know it. As I strolled along the shore, water lapping at my ankles, I remember slowing my pace and turning to face the vast, blue ocean. The water seemed to still, and the noise of the people around me faded. That's when I heard the whisper, *"Jodi, can you be available for what I want to do in your life? Can you be open to having a child?"* I was stunned. Chills cascaded down my arms and legs. Did I hear God right? Surely not. Why would He ask me that now when I was finally fulfilling my lifelong dream of being a television news anchor?

When I returned to work that evening, I felt a deep restlessness settle into my soul. I could not shake the questions God asked me during that beach encounter. At first, I shoved God's request way down, busying myself, trying to ignore it. I threw even more effort, time, and energy into my work. I even volunteered to work extra shifts. After all, I had labored so diligently to secure my job. Surely, God supported this. I reminded myself that I had never really dreamed of having children, and doctors had told me that because of a medical condition, it might be extremely difficult to get pregnant. But God was chasing after me. He would not let me be, especially at night when He would interrupt my sleep, waking me in the hush of the night quietly whispering, *"Jodi, what is your answer? Can you be open to what I want to do through you and D.J.? Do you trust me?"* God was lighting a tiny spark and calling to my feminine heart.

My heart was troubled. I took my concerns and distress directly to the Lord. I wrestled with Him through intense prayer, pleading my case and clawing at my independence. But through studying His Holy Scriptures and intentional conversation with God on my knees, I became confident about what God was asking me, even if it didn't make sense. Clinging to control and my career guided my head, but God was calling my heart. I would learn firsthand that surrendering what I desired professionally to God's proposal to give my time and energy where I mattered most was beautifully reckless and eternally rewarding. God was summoning me to lay down my job to give my best to my husband because he was getting my leftovers. He was inviting me to surrender my need for independence to be available to His plan for opening my womb because God was calling me to become a mother. His invitation surprised me because motherhood had not been part of my plan. I had longed for a career. But I could not ignore the uneasiness I felt in my soul. God was disrupting my life, disrupting the peace in my soul because He was longing to capture my entire heart. God was chasing me down and asking me to trust Him with my fertility and His will for my life, even if accepting His invitation would mean my life would look differently than I had imagined.

That day, I rolled my shoulders back and looked Dawn square in the eyes, afraid she might glimpse the fear I held underneath but sure I was following God's call on my life. It marked a turning point in my life. I chose to walk away from where I was *replaceable* to serve first and best where I was most *irreplaceable*. It was the scariest and best decision I'd ever had to make. Throughout my life, this would become a critical crossroad I would reencounter again and again.

Perhaps today, God is inviting you to do the same. To choose to pour your best effort, time, and love into where you matter the most.

Just this morning, I opened my phone, and the words scratched colorfully across my social media stories made me stop scrolling Instagram. *"I am hiring a full-time Nanny...because I am so overwhelmed!"* My finger swiped the screen, and I saw a picture of this beautiful dark-haired woman, Becky, made famous by her recent stint on the hit reality show *The Bachelorette,* lying exhausted on the couch. She was flanked by a breast pump and a pile of paperwork, her assistant holding her baby in the background. Becky explained (in colorful font sprawled over more pictures in her social media stories) that she was balancing raising two kids under three, a modeling job, her travel schedule, her social life, and a new business venture. She said she simply had no more patience for breastfeeding, and her toddler was "draining her energy." She was weary, and rightfully so. Something had to give for her to get it all done, and assigning the care of her kids to someone else seemed like the best solution. She was ready to take her "life back" (her words, not mine).

I sat my phone down on our kitchen countertop, and my heart sank. Because do you know what I saw? Something way too familiar. A young mother with an unsettled heart stuck between her professional ambitions, her dreams, and the needs of small children. Desperate and overworked, she was reaching out to social media for permission to delegate her mothering responsibilities when what she needed was a reorientation of her life's priorities. She was searching for wisdom from the wrong source. What she needed was encouragement and a reminder of why her dedication to raising her own children mattered in a monumental way. I saw a mama who was so caught up in everything she wanted to accomplish that she was neglecting where she was most needed.

I saw...myself.

This is how I felt years ago before I learned how irreplaceable my presence is in my children's lives. This Bachelorette, who had previously shared with *People* magazine about her heartbreaking struggle with infertility and her desire to become a mother, believed she was... replaceable. I wanted to reach through that iPhone to tell her she was mistaken! Her personal motherhood has profound significance in her children's lives, especially in their earliest and most formative years.

I'm so grateful I learned the value of my commitment to raising my children when they were still small enough to be nestled in my arms.

Motherhood is a sacred topic to me because, for a time, when my children were little, I mothered with a divided heart, feeling the constant tug between pursuing what I craved to accomplish and the energy and attention small children require. After the birth of my first two daughters, something miraculously shifted, birthing the message of this book. But this learning was a painful process, wrecking the expectations and dreams of what I thought my life would look like. As I spent time studying God's Word, the rich stories of the Christian saints, and the scientific data touting the significant role a mother plays in her child's life, I began to understand more clearly why I was sensing a deep urge to spend my best energy and give my whole heart to motherhood. Although it was counter-cultural, God was inviting me to lean into where I am most irreplaceable. If you have small children, He is offering you the same invitation today.

Are you struggling with your role as a mother? Are you feeling so overwhelmed by the responsibility of caring for little ones? Uncertain of how to prioritize it all? Do you desire to pour your heart into work outside the home but feel guilty when you are away? Do you secretly feel like you are not cut out to raise your own children, and they are far better off with someone else looking after them during the day so that you can fulfill your own personal purpose? You are not alone. I see you sister.

We are at a point in history when more U.S. women are skipping motherhood today than ever [2]. The Pew Research Center says the growing trend is for women to delay motherhood, spend more time in the labor force than in the past, and spend more time and money on child care. [3]. With parenting pundits telling us raising children means "more responsibilities and less me-time" [4], it is no wonder 77% of women admit motherhood overwhelms them and they feel "a lot of pressure to be an involved parent" [5]. When we look around at how motherhood is often depicted on social media and in movies, we can become easily deflated about our roles as mothers.

Author Carrie Gress says the last few decades of women embracing radical feminism has placed motherhood on the chopping block, making motherhood appear "dispensable." [6] Gress writes, "It can be no accident that we are witnessing unprecedented emotional and mental trauma and brokenness in every segment of our population because motherhood has been so devalued and neglected." [7]

In today's culture, mothers hear the message that devoting themselves to motherhood and the shepherding of their children is not enough. We are told we must cultivate our careers, build our brands, be noticed for our accomplishments, and have a stellar social media handle. The message to women is deafening: We must *do* something with our lives, or else we will become outdated. Dare I say, it is easy to believe that if we pour our first and best energy into motherhood, we risk becoming forgotten. Motherhood can feel like a season to rush through to get to a more important season where we can live our best life.

"The implication," writes Allison Ciraulo in her beautiful piece *Motherhood as a Path to Sainthood,* is that "work in the home and the care of children is not desirable or enjoyable in and of itself and does not allow a woman the space she needs to flourish and live as a whole person, constrained as she is by all the menial tasks that consume her days, her months, and her years. The message women get is that they must be a mother *and* something else, or risk becoming irrelevant." [8]

Our society neglects to address the prominent role mothers play in their children's lives. This oversight will have a devastating impact on future generations. We need a reorientation. That's where my story comes in. I want to change the narrative.

It's time to radically reverse our society's messaging to mothers. Instead of motherhood being labeled obsolete and unnecessary, we need to showcase its significance. Instead of our children getting our leftover energy and time, we need to prioritize them. Boldly parading the significance of a woman's role in her child's life in today's heightened cultural climate is controversial but necessary. Motherhood can not be erased.

Mothers balance so many jobs. We are short-order cooks. Chemists. Nurturers. Breadwinners. Science Fair Supporters. Carpool drivers. Target runners. Chemists. Bank tellers. Team Moms and coaches and cheerleaders. We are late-night laundry folders and the finders of all things lost. We are experts at tightening swim goggles and applying sunscreen to screaming toddlers. Mothers are teen therapists. We are our children's first and finest teachers. Mothers are warriors. We are brave. We jump in to rescue our children, even when it will cost us everything.

Today's mothers are asked to juggle so many roles that we often lose sight of what is most important: our influence on our children. Motherhood is accepting a divine invitation. It is answering *yes* to God's appeal to trust Him. It says *yes* to understanding and living how God designed our feminine spirit.

Are you wrestling with your role as a mother? Are you trying to balance it all, squeezing in parenting around all of the other things you tackle on a daily basis? Do you feel torn between what you want to get done or accomplish and caring for the people in your home? For years, I did.

My personal transformation happened when I discovered the key essence of motherhood, not from what the current culture touts it to be, but what our Creator God desires it to be. I had to seek out how God says we should approach the "reward" of shepherding children. But I had to first *see* my little ones as a reward! God calls children a "gift" and a "heritage." (Psalm 127:3). Things radically shifted in my life's priorities when I better understood God's design and intention for the feminine heart and motherhood. Once I embraced the principle of what author and mothering coach Holly Pierlot so bravely teaches, "We have a real, important, irreplaceable mission - a *personal mission* to raise our children," [9] my lens of motherhood wholly changed.

This would not happen overnight.

Realizing how pivotal my mothering role was in my children's lives was a painful lesson because it demanded I make some life changes to prioritize raising my children. It has meant cutting back or laying aside many of my desires so I can be fully available to give my best energy, time, and affection to cultivate this treasure from God, my children. I want to pause and be clear here. Elevating motherhood does not downgrade women's personal passions and giftedness, which God has placed on our hearts, nor should it. To be good mothers, we need to be whole women first. Whole women are secure in knowing who they are and that their core worth can not come singularly from motherhood. Motherhood is a high and sacred calling, but it is not our chief identity. God invites us to find our core worth in the truth that we are His beloved daughters.

But I believe God is inviting us to flip what our culture says upside down by first applying our giftedness and talent, our ambitions and purpose, in our children's lives before we offer the best parts of ourselves to the world. He wants our passions to complement our motherhood, not compete with it. God desires us to see the significance our purposeful presence and love has in our children's lives. C.S. Lewis says caring for the people and the needs in our homes is "the most important work in the world...your job is the one for which all others exist." [10] Before I was enlightened about the value of motherhood, this sentiment used to make me cringe, but now I wholeheartedly agree.

"There is a strong case to be made for full-time, wholehearted motherhood - and this is something women rarely hear anymore," as Sally Clarkson says in her book *The Mission of Motherhood*. [11] It is time to re-ignite the conversation about motherhood. Your decision to mother your own children matters.

In practicality, this looks different for each of us. This book is not about waging a battle between stay-at-home mamas and working ones. Life is not that simple. Some of us have to earn a paycheck to make ends meet. Each family has unique circumstances. But this is about reminding us we always have a choice, and we often need encouragement to take ownership of our own lives. We get to decide how to structure our hours and what and whom to prioritize. And ultimately, making those decisions boils down to what we believe is most important today.

Motherhood is not just a job; it is a vocation. Raising our children well, cultivating their self-esteem, caring for their physical bodies, and shepherding their emotional and spiritual hearts is not something we can do on the side, secondary to our personal careers. If we have the honor of having children, I now believe motherhood is the highest, most honorable lifework.

In his *Letter to Families*, Pope John Paul II says, "Raising children can be considered a genuine apostolate." [12] The Christian church says a vocation is a call. The word 'vocation' comes from the Latin *vocatio*, which means 'calling.' A vocation is an invitation from God –His call- to each person to love and serve Him and His Church in a particular state or way of life. A vocation is becoming the woman God is calling me to be. [13] The Catholic Church says we all have a "Universal call [*vocatio*] to holiness in the Church." [14]

St. Paul talks about our vocations in the Holy Scriptures, in Ephesians, by begging us to "walk in a manner worthy of the *calling* to which you have been *called*." He urges us to tackle this with "all lowliness, meekness, with patience, forbearing one another in love." (Ephesians 4:1 -2)

The vocation of motherhood is not a prison sentence. It is a privilege. It is a heavenly invitation to serve uniquely where only you can. Your child can only have one mother, and that is you. Your calling is exclusive; it is particular to you. Pope Francis says the Lord's call is not an "intrusion on our freedom" nor a "cage" or "burden to be borne." Instead, it is "a loving initiative whereby God encounters us and invites us to be part of a great undertaking." [15]

God wants to use your story of motherhood as a testimony of His love for you. Catholic Theologian Peter Kreeft said, "All of our most beautiful stories are like the Gospel: they are tragedies first, and then comedies; they are crosses and then crowns. They are crosses because they are conflicts between good and evil. That is the fundamental plot of every great story. To say "that story is beautiful" means "that story resembles the Gospel." [16] Our commitment to motherhood is an incredible calling to share the Gospel.

I pray that my words spark a dialogue between you and God as you take inventory of your heart. So, today, I have a question for you. Do you feel a quiet tug that God is summoning you to give more energy and time to mothering the very souls He has placed into your care, but do you feel uncertain you have what it takes? If you are blessed with having children, I would argue that if you can quiet your heart and listen closely enough, the answer is a resounding yes. God is calling you to be the best mother you can be. God has gifted you your children. You are not matched by accident. He is assigning them to your care. 1 Corinthians 7:17 says, "Only, let every one lead the life which the Lord has *assigned* to him, and in which God has *called* him." (emphasis mine). The time to be "all-in" and embrace God's calling to motherhood is now. Do not waste another day.

As a mother, you have an irreplaceable role in your child's life. God wants to use you as His instrument to cultivate your son or daughter's heart. There is no greater mission than accepting God's invitation to shepherd a human soul. Your discipleship in mothering has eternal value. As I share how God called me to fully embrace my role as a mother and the principles that have anchored my commitment to giving my first and best energy to raising my children, I pray you will hear Him calling you also. This book can be your field guide. A supernatural peace comes when we lean into loving where we matter the most. How will you respond to His holy invitation?

2

Igniting A Desire

> *"She who guarded in her heart the secret of divine maternity was the first to see the face of God made man in the tiny fruit of her womb."*
> Pope Benedict XVI

When I discovered I was pregnant, relief and exhilaration washed over me. How faithful God had been! I called my husband and asked him to meet me under the limbs of a giant willow tree on my parents' Maryland farm. It was there that I told my high-school sweetheart and best friend I was carrying his first child. The joy I saw on D.J.'s face is etched in my memory forever. In total amazement, we cried and praised God for this miracle and His sovereign plan.

It had been six months since we had started giving our bodies fully to each other without any limitations. The love welling up between us was overflowing. There was no barrier between us now. We were giving ourselves to each other freely and openly. It was a beautiful time in our marriage.

Ironically, just one week before I took a positive pregnancy test, my husband and I had been brainstorming with our doctor about how we could get pregnant. After reviewing my menstrual chart, the doctor suggested I probably had not ovulated for months. All too familiar with my personal irregular menstrual cycle, I had been prepared (and warned by specialists) that pregnancy would not come quickly for me. The doctor recommended various drugs we could use to help me ovulate, but both my husband and I were not ready to try any of those yet. We left her office with a prescription for a drug that would make me bleed and clean out the lining of my uterus. The goal was to hopefully restart my cycle. What we didn't know (doctor included) is that during that very visit...I was already pregnant! The doctor was so convinced that pregnancy would be difficult for me she didn't even have me take a test, and I naively didn't push to have one.

As we left the OB's office, my husband and I thought her recommendation sounded like a good idea. Days later, when I went to pick up the prescription, I heard this tiny voice in my soul cautioning me to wait to take it. I told my husband this, and we prayed it over. Then, I threw the prescription in the trash. That uneasy nudge I had felt was undoubtedly from the Holy Spirit, and thank goodness we listened because taking the medicine would have aborted that precious new life just beginning in my womb. When I learned of our pregnancy, I fell to my knees, thanking God He had warned me not to take the medicine. I felt honored to carry a baby and was amazed that God had gifted us this pregnancy so quickly.

When I was twelve weeks pregnant, our Doctor moved closer to the sonogram screen and squinted. We were ecstatic and nervous to hear our baby's heartbeat. But I could tell from the doctor's face as she conducted my sonogram that something was off. The doctor paused and then turned the screen away from us. She leaned in closer to get a better look at the picture. I wasn't prepared for the grief of what would come when she told us the news that our baby had stopped growing some weeks ago. There was a small amniotic sac and some tissue where a new life had started to form, but no longer a heartbeat. She told us we needed to prepare for a miscarriage, and if I didn't start bleeding naturally, the doctor recommended a D and C as soon as possible. I heard nothing she said after that. I have never cried so hard in my life.

The car ride home was a blur. Grandparents, waiting for exciting phone calls, were met with heartbreaking sobs. This baby was from the Lord. We just knew it. And God had already spared this new life once when I didn't take that prescription to clean out my uterus. Right? Why did God save this baby once to then take him or her away from us? It felt so cruel. And it made no sense. This was the wrong ending. I wanted to rewrite the story.

And I was so used to doing that. In the newsroom, when a script line didn't look or sound right, I could correct it right on the spot. I was good at improvising. Making things right. But the fact that our baby had stopped growing and was no longer alive? I was helpless, no matter how much I wanted to change the facts. I had never felt so out of control in my life.

The grief was unbearable. The baby was due in November. We had already started dreaming about what Thanksgiving and Christmas would be like with a newborn. We had logged late nights batting around baby names. My breasts were swollen and tender, and I had already started collecting books about the pros and cons of breastfeeding.

After the devastating news, we waited almost two weeks, praying for a miracle. After another round of ultrasounds showed no change and still no heartbeat, we consented to the D and C. Friends told me that I would be relieved when the procedure was over and that I would be able to move on. Instead, I will never forget how my entire soul ached with grief as the anesthesia wore off. I had a throbbing pelvis, evidence of what had been ripped away. Hours later, we turned into the driveway of our sleepy town with an empty womb and grieving hearts. Our baby was gone. My husband lifted me from the car and carried me to our bedroom. He lay beside me in our bed. And I wept. And wept. And wept.

As I was healing, I remember waking up in the middle of the night with a pulsating fear that perhaps if I had wanted this baby more, God would have let me keep him. I was hurt and confused. Was this my fault? This is what God had asked me to give up my career in television for? This suffering? Maybe I just wasn't cut out for this anyway. Why would God have asked me to open myself up to become a mother, allow me to get pregnant under extraordinary circumstances, and then take this baby away? I confided in God how hurt I was and how He had let me down. I heard His voice whisper, "*I can handle your disappointment, Jodi. Bring me your hurt. I am crying right alongside you. I'm still asking that you trust me. Stay with me. I am by your side.*"

I remember telling God that my heart was bruised beyond repair. Psalm 34:18 kept ringing in my mind, "The Lord is near to the brokenhearted and saves those who are crushed in spirit."

I sensed this suffering was doing an incredible work in my heart. Suddenly, I was curious about other women's fertility struggles when I had previously been oblivious. I thought back to a time when I interviewed a woman who had buried a stillborn baby. How my heart ached for her now! I remembered the co-worker who was in constant anguish because she could not get pregnant and the friend who was still haunted by the horrific decision to abort her baby when she was just a teen. I wept for those women, now understanding just a sliver of the pain they have been through in losing a child. It was as if the crushing pain of losing a baby was taking the blinders off of my eyes by allowing me to see other's suffering.

"The best things in life are the result of being wounded," writes Frederick William Robertson. "Wheat must be crushed before becoming bread, and incense must be burned by fire before its fragrance is set free. The earth must be broken with a sharp plow before being ready to receive the seed. And it is a broken heart that pleases God." [1]

Weeks after the baby was gone, I woke up in the middle of the night and stumbled downstairs. I opened up my Bible to the Gospel of St. Luke, and as I read her story, I turned to a fresh page in my journal to record her words. The angel of the Lord visited Mary with an unusual and scandalous request. God was inviting her to be a vessel of the world's Savior. In Luke 1:30, the angel said, "Behold, you will conceive in your womb and bear a son, and you shall call his name Jesus." The Scriptures tell us that Mary was greatly troubled (verse 29) but was willing. "And Mary said, "Behold I am a handmaid of the Lord; let it be to me according to your word." (verse 38) I researched the word *handmaid*. It means servant, helper, assistant, dependent.

Following this incredible mother's heart, I learned Mary's "yes" had no limits. She was all in. She loved the Lord and wanted to do His will, even if it meant her entire town was whispering words of scandal behind her back. Mary's "yes" was given before she knew what her "fiat" would require. Her "yes" was given to love before she knew the ache of who she would be asked to surrender. Her "yes" was given, and that "yes" gave a fallen world the gift of a Savior. Mary was willing to mother Jesus Christ of Nazareth. Jesus, both fully divine and fully man, would come to die on the Cross and rise from the dead for the redemption of all mankind. Mary's "yes" allowed God to open the gates of heaven through the gift of His only Son, Jesus. I leaned into the courage of Mary and took solace in her full trust in God and His sovereign plan. Luke 2:51 tells us that Mary "kept all these things" the Lord taught her and "pondered them in her heart."

Through the example of Mary, we have a picture of womanhood at its pinnacle, an untainted vessel full of grace carrying the light of Christ out into the world. [2] Author Colleen C. Mitchell says God invites us to live pregnant with the same hope Mary had. She invites, "God dwelling in me can unfold into a grace and salvation of God active in me, as Mary was the moment she heard the angel's greeting sound in her ears." [3]

In those months of healing, other stories from the Bible and the lives of the Saints seemed to come alive in a new way. I sought comfort from the men and women in the Holy Scriptures who had been transformed by their earthly suffering. Many had experienced significant loss. I was in good company in my suffering.

"God is inviting us not to do more, but become more," writes Ruth Schwenk. "I can't help but think of some of the difficulties the people of God faced when He called them to fulfill His purposes. Abraham left his tribal homeland. Moses led Israel out of slavery in Egypt. Esther saved a nation by asking for the favor of a king who held her life and the lives of her people in his hands. Nehemiah left a palace to restore a city in ruins. Noah confronted a corrupt city.

All of it was hard, risky, sacrificial work. But it was the type of work that mattered. In every example, God was doing a good work. He was changing lives, redirecting generations, altering outcomes, and restoring what had been destroyed. It was hard work because it mattered. God was accomplishing His purposes, pushing back darkness with His shining light. The mess is where God wants to meet us. Not to stay there but to grow there. What I love about each of these stories is not just what God did with these faithful acts of obedience. I love that in every story, the men and women involved were not just used by God. They were forever changed by God. God had given them more than they could handle, but He didn't ask them to handle it alone." [4]

Alice von Hildebrand, a Catholic philosopher and theologian, calls on women to change the world by embracing feminine virtues. These often were best developed through intense suffering. "Woman by her very nature is maternal - for every woman, whether...married or unmarried, is called upon to be a biological, psychological or spiritual mother - she knows intuitively that to give, to nurture, to care for others, to suffer with and for them - for maternity implies suffering - is infinitely more valuable in God's sight than to conquer nations and fly to the moon," said von Hildebrand.

I started to see the tragedy of losing our first baby as an opportunity to do greater spiritual work in my soul. Suffering was leading me into a deeper relationship with Jesus Christ. Robertson adds, "If you aspire to be a person of consolation, if you want to share the priestly gift of sympathy, if you desire to go beyond giving commonplace comfort to a heart that is tempted, and if you long to go through the daily exchanges of life with the kind of tact that never inflicts pain, then you must be prepared to pay the price for a costly education - for like Christ, you must suffer." [5]

I had opened my life up to motherhood, and my heart had been wounded. But something even more unbelievable happened to me; my suffering had softened my heart. For the first time, I acknowledged a deep, hidden longing to raise a child. God used a taste of tragedy to ignite a new desire in my soul. But I kept this new dream a secret, even from my husband, out of fear it might never come true.

How would you describe your own path to motherhood? Perhaps pregnancy came sooner than you expected, and you are now faced with many uncertainties and a radical life shift that you had not planned on. Maybe you are reading this today feeling desperate for one more child, pushing down the ache of seeing other friends get pregnant so easily when nothing seems to be going the way you had dreamed. Or it could be you are already mothering a house full of kids. Yet, you feel a gentle whisper from God asking you to be open to one more child when you can not fathom taking on more responsibility. My friend, Jesus sees you in all of this. He knows your story, your heartache, your fear, your pain. Jesus sits alongside you and wants you to lean on Him for comfort and direction. He longs for you to bring your uncertainty, frustration, and discomfort. Open your heart to Him today. Confide in Him. Let Him in. Give Him all of your desires. You can trust Him.

3

A Priestly Revelation For Motherhood

> *"The discernment of vocation is above all the fruit of an intimate dialogue between the Lord and his disciples."*
>
> Pope Benedict XVI

Months after I lost my first baby, I was on my lunch break from work when I noticed a woman and her child sitting nearby. He was maybe two, sitting on her lap as she caressed his hair and rocked him back and forth. This Mama was enamored with this little boy, and I could see why. He was simply delightful. As I studied them closer, I clutched my abdomen, still freshly grieving the loss of our baby. Watching this mother's tenderness with her son made my eyes sting with tears. She was taken with him. He was clearly a gift from God. At that moment, for the first time in my life, I felt a deep yearning to ask God for a child. I wanted to share *that* sacred desire with my husband. I wanted to learn to open myself up to greater love. **I wanted to become a mother.**

God, in His graciousness, heard my desire. He also had a sense of humor. From the moment the doctor confirmed our next baby had a heartbeat and was healthy, I threw up. I vomited at work, during Mass, before and after dinner. I had my husband frantically pull the car over so I could throw up over the guardrails of a buzzing interstate (not safe, but when in doubt, always do what a pregnant woman screams at you to do). I lost the contents of my stomach when I glanced at someone else's meal. At the end of my first trimester, we went on a cruise with my husband's extended family (I do not recommend this when you are ridiculously nauseous already). Everyone on vacation had a lovely time (or so I heard). I wouldn't know because I spent the entire trip with my head over a toilet bowl, quarantined in our room.

By the time my stomach settled down, I was well into my third trimester and flustered over what to do with my time when this baby arrived. I was blessed that I had options when so many others do not because of my husband's career. We had decided to live off of one income from the beginning of our marriage, stowing away any salary I made into savings. The possibilities for what I should do clouded my mind. Should I find a part-time television news job? Maybe write for a newspaper? Pursue a different career? Stay home full-time?

While wrestling over what type of mother I wanted to be when this baby arrived, one particular conversation with my husband stood out. "It is up to you, Jo," D.J. told me one afternoon as we strolled the trail near our house, "But I think you would be a fantastic full-time mother. I know your heart, and I think you would love to be around for our children's big and small moments. Do you remember what I said when I married you? I just knew you would be an incredible mother to my children." Although I hated to admit it (humility is my husband's spiritual gift, not mine), I knew deep down he had nailed what resonated quietly in my heart. God was inviting me to give my best energy to raise this baby. But there was one problem. I was scared stiff. I knew I was good at working in the newsroom but felt utterly unprepared to be a mother. What in the heck would I do all at home with an infant when I thrived in a fast-paced work environment with adults?

Although I had yet to meet our baby, I was sick over the thought of working full-time and leaving her in the care of someone else. I didn't want to miss out on my baby's first moments. I wanted her to feel loved and seen. I desired her to feel cherished and prioritized. But I desired a career, too. The baby hadn't even arrived yet, and I already felt stuck between two strong drives. One led to pursuing what *I* wanted, the other to giving my full self to the care of someone else. I was petrified that choosing motherhood full-time would keep me housebound, hiding my gifts and talents. I scratched out in my journal, "*God... what do you want me to do? This doesn't make sense. I have prepared my entire life for a career. I have studied, worked, and pushed. I have so much to accomplish and do for you, God! Why would I hide away at home to care for one child when I can make a big difference in this world?*" These questions haunted me as my belly grew larger each day.

During these same months, my husband and I met weekly with a small group to grow our knowledge and faith in the Catholic Church. My husband was a devout Catholic, and God was calling me to convert, but I had so many questions. We were led by a priest who was on fire for God. Father Eric Arnold was young, intelligent, and handsome. A deep, passionate love for Jesus Christ radiated out of him, and he was patient and purposeful in answering my questions about the Catholic faith. As the weeks passed and we got to know him better, I remember thinking Father Arnold would have made a fabulous husband. Why didn't he marry? Surely he must battle daily with his decision to become a priest? I just had to ask. Father Arnold's answer shook me.

"Yes, Jodi, I did really want to get married," he confided. Confused, I pushed him further. "Then what happened? Surely that desire disappeared when you took your vow, and that's why it was a simple decision to follow God's calling into full-time service of the Church? God just took that desire away?" The beautiful peace radiating from his face told me that he meant what he was about to say next.

"My desire to marry never really went completely away, but my desire to follow God's will became the strongest pull in my life. In my late twenties, God called me to the priesthood. My hunger for marriage diminished in the shadow of my desire to serve Christ where He can use me best. Being a priest is my primary call from God. The rest is a distant second. When God gifts us a vocation, He always supplies the grace and strength to live that calling out."

I was dumbfounded. Father Arnold pursued a deep relationship with Jesus Christ. He found His call to the priesthood stronger than his desire to marry. He allowed God to use him and his deep love of the sacraments to strengthen marriages like mine and bring converts to the Church. Witnessing Father Arnold fulfill his personal calling was a beautiful witness of the Gospel. He was serving where he was most irreplaceable. Perhaps God was inviting me to do the same?

For the next few weeks, Father Arnold's words keep rushing through my head. God was giving us a child. How would we treat this beautiful gift? After suffering a miscarriage, I understood the sacredness of new life. This precious little one was gaining strength daily in my womb. He or she already knew my voice. This baby represented the love between my husband and me. It reflected our willingness to give ourselves entirely to each other. This new life echoed the love of our Sovereign God.

Would the Creator of this child really want someone else to raise him or her for forty-plus hours a week while I headed off to work? He entrusted this baby to me, but did it really matter if I was with him or her most of the day? Should I give up all sense of myself to stay home and raise this baby? I was unsettled.

During this time, I poured myself into deep conversation with God through prayer. I consulted His love letter, the Holy Scriptures, for guidance. My time studying the Holy Scriptures initially brought a deeper sense of uneasiness to my heart. God did not want a part of me, He wanted ALL of me. I learned that God offers His people a life of inner peace. If I wanted to find peace of heart, I needed to allow Him to capture my whole heart. God was disrupting my life, unsettling my soul, because He had a message for me. He was inviting me to be open to His will. God needed to quiet my soul so that I could discern His whisper.

In *Searching For and Maintaining Peace,* Father Jacques Philippe writes, "God does not speak and does not operate except in peace, not in trouble and agitation. Let us remember the experience of the prophet Elijah of Horeb: God was not in the hurricane, nor the earthquake, nor in the fire, but in the whisper of a gentle breeze (1 Kings 19)." [1]

Once again, I discovered my soul was agitated and disturbed because I was insistent on pushing my agenda and my independence. God was calling me to gaze on Him and allow His love, wisdom, and power to work through me by being open to carrying new life. **God**

was inviting me to be available to Him. I had a choice in how I would respond.

As I spent weeks combing over Scripture and pouring my heart out to God, I encountered the stories of spiritual powerhouses who faced similar predicaments as mine. God had asked them to be open to His will and granted them free choice on how they would reply. But one story stood out.

Perhaps you know my buddy Abraham well. But if not, let me give you a "teaser" (as we news reporters call it) to get you up to speed. God told Abram in Genesis 12 that he would do great things for God's name through his and his wife Sarai's descendants (God would lengthen Abram's name later and change his wife's name to Sarah). There was only one slight problem. Sarai's womb was as barren as the desert they lived in (cheesy, yes, but true). And that's when Abram got the "call," which just didn't make sense. God asked Abram to leave his homeland in Ur of the Chaldeans and travel to a land God would show him. Leaving like this was not part of Abram's "life" plan. In fact, this move was highly inconvenient.

Abraham learned that obedience to God requires trust. Personal obedience to God's request is often not popular among the people in your circle. Obedience is sometimes costly. To obey means you may feel left out, left behind, or sometimes an alien among your own people. My guess is Abraham surely did.

I believed that obedience to God's invitation to open my womb and raise a child could cost me all I had worked so hard to get. Abraham's example showed me that obeying wholeheartedly without knowing what is up around the bend is okay. Abraham obeyed all the way. Right away. With his whole heart. And God blessed him abundantly. God was faithful to what He promised He would do beyond what Abraham had the understanding to fathom. But Abraham had to be willing to say, "Here I am Lord. Use me as you wish."

During this time of discernment, one verse kept resonating with my heart. I taped Hebrews 11:8 to the inside of our kitchen cabinet. I read it every morning before work, "By faith Abraham, when called to go to a place he would later receive as his inheritance, obeyed and went, even though he did not know where he was going."

Even though Abraham was uncertain where God was calling him or what he would find when he arrived, he obeyed God and went. Obedience and trust. That was what God had asked of Abraham and what He was asking from me. As I kept unpacking the Bible and studying the teachings of the Church, I learned that the acts of obedience and trust are the secret of the saints and the key to following Jesus Christ. We trust God because He gave us the gift of His only Son so that we might have access to spending eternity with Him. We obey God because we love Him and are grateful for His sacrifice. We obey God because we can trust God.

1 John 4:9-10 says, "This is how God's love was revealed among us: God sent His one and only Son into the world, so that we might live through Him. And love consists in this: not that we loved God, but that He loved us and sent His Son as the atoning sacrifice for our sins."

Are you wrestling over something, unsure which way to turn or what to do? All of us have seasons where our hearts wrestle with deep questions. Once we identify these struggles, we can invite God to guide us in discernment. We have an invitation to surrender our battle to Him. In what ways is God asking you to trust Him more, particularly as a mother?

God was calling me to something more. The restlessness I felt had a remedy. God asked me to be available and allow His will to work through my life, but I felt uncertain about how to respond. Things would become much more apparent to me during the dark morning hours of an early April day. I would awake from my sleep to find that a new life was coming. God was calling me to abandon myself and my "life" plans to motherhood, and He was about to get my answer in how I would respond.

4

A Divine Privilege

"Jo, you look like you've been in a fight!" My younger brother Jimmy bent over the hospital bed and kissed the top of my head. My hair was still matted down from sweat. I was draped in a (delightfully flattering) hospital gown, and I grimaced every time I had to shift my body to move - my pelvis pulsating from the just-hours-old stitching. I couldn't turn my neck to the left side because it was knotted in pain. But the worst part was my eyes. Even I did a double take when I looked at my reflection in the hospital bathroom mirror. The pushing I endured during my first labor and delivery had been so long and so fierce that I had broken multiple blood vessels around my face, leaving red streaks across the whites of my eyes. So much for the beautiful pictures women share on social media just hours after birthing a baby! I felt like I fit better in a horror film!

And this would have been a blockbuster. For the past twenty-four hours, I had been trying to push someone out of my body, who I had no idea how to…push out. This little bundle of joy was obviously in no hurry to meet me because our baby was doing nothing to cooperate in her voyage down my birth canal.

Our little one had begun the journey to meet us in the middle of the night, a little before 2 am. I awoke, curled under the covers beside my husband, surprised to find I had "wet" the bed (a first for me!) My due date was still two weeks away, and I silently scolded myself for chugging a big glass of water before nightfall as I begrudgingly waddled to the bathroom to change my clothes. As I sat down, water gushed from my pelvis and into the toilet. I was shocked! What was going on here? I stood up and tried to peer past my belly. What I saw made me call out to my husband. A clear, warm, water-like substance was dripping from me onto the floor. And suddenly, a massive smile swept across my face. My water had broken! I was in labor!

Wanting to labor at home as long as I could, I convinced my husband to fall back asleep so I could ready some things. In the darkness, I floated around in total joy, anticipating meeting our baby for the first time. The house was quiet and still. I savored the hours of precious time alone with the Lord before I would meet our baby. As I threw in a load of laundry of baby blankets and tiny clothes, I petitioned God for comfort and asked Him for strength. I smiled so wide as I wondered, would our bundle be a boy or a girl? As we waited, would God whisper a new baby name that had escaped our shortlist? I did not even consider lying down to sleep. I was too excited. I packed my hospital bag, took a hot shower, washed and curled my hair, and wrote God a long letter in my prayer journal, relishing in the final hours of my pregnancy. My words on the page poured out, thanking God for the gift of carrying this precious child. As morning approached and the sun peaked into the nearby sky, I slipped outside to walk our long farmhouse driveway. It would be my last time alone before my life was changed. My contractions were slow and steady. Our baby was on the way.

In an attempt to give our little one the best "serene birth experience" (this is actually written out in my birth plan, people, the one that I typed, hole-punched, and color-coded offered to the nurses upon my arrival to the hospital. Lord, have mercy on me). I labored at home until about lunchtime, and then when I was admitted, I sacrificially refused all drugs, wanting nothing to come between me and my baby. I was determined to give birth naturally. I wanted my baby to be as alert and healthy as possible and didn't want her first breath to be clouded by any side-effects of drugs that might be running through my system. If my own Mama could do it, so could I.

I have been through a lot of physical strain and surgery since that day, but let's set the record straight right here my friend. Listen up, now. There is nothing, nothing, as painful as natural childbirth. If you don't believe me, then may God bless you (and you are no longer my friend).

After pushing for two and half hours (and maybe some quiet cussing?- some details are foggy, ask my husband), I overheard the doctor say I might need a C-Section to get the baby out. Exhausted, I remember that I couldn't even see straight. And that I wanted a refund on the $150 we spent on that ridiculous natural laboring class. The instructor, who told me to remain calm and quiet while a human person pushed her way out of my unmentionable area, clearly was a lunatic. I was short on time and low on energy. I had to get this baby out naturally.

Except I couldn't.

And that's when the scissors and then the vacuum came out. After I refused all drugs, our doctor turned on the switch and tugged on the vacuum's gray, snake-like attachment. And with what little muster I had left, I braced my body for impact as that vacuum whizzed and sucked our daughter out of my body and into this world. Oh, the glories of motherhood.

Nothing could have prepared me for the horrors of my first labor and delivery. But I also wasn't prepared for something else: the explosion of love that flooded my heart the first time our little girl nestled snugly onto my bare chest. Welcoming our precious daughter, Lillian, wrecked me. I was undone with emotion and devotion to this eight-pound bundle of screaming joy. Yes, she had almost killed me coming out. But within minutes of meeting her, she was instantly forgiven. I was completely surprised by my instant connection with her, the fierce awareness that I had been entrusted with a living, breathing gift.

My first lesson in how irreplaceable I was as a mother came quickly. From our first encounter, Lilli turned her face toward mine, opening her mouth, longing to be fed. Our baby was active, alert, her eyes searching for support and comfort. She was hungry, and she looked to me for nourishment. I was amazed. I had decided to give breastfeeding a try but was prepared to bottle-feed if that was best for my baby. After all, the thought of another human sucking milk out of my breast seemed totally foreign to me. But to my surprise, when our baby nestled to my breast, it wasn't strange; it was beautiful.

As the experts came by to visit our room, it became clear the nourishment from my own breast was an enormous benefit for my baby. I was astounded at how God had designed the milk that would flow from my breast with just the proper nutrients for what she needed. How miraculous to discover that although a newborn has poor eyesight, she can focus on what is about 9-12 inches away. That's the very distance between a baby's eyes and her mother's when she is held in the crook of her mother's arm.

Although, for various reasons, not every woman can breastfeed her child (any new Mama who tells you breastfeeding is not quite challenging and even painful at times needs to sit for a lie detector test), I was convinced to give it my best shot after learning of its innumerable benefits. What I am about to share here is not meant to make you feel inferior if you have chosen to not breastfeed your baby because, as I mentioned before, you purposefully hold and cuddle your baby near your face. At the same time, you feed him so he can gaze into your loving eyes. It has the tremendous benefit of building his feeling of security and attachment. But I needed persuasion to breastfeed, and you might too. Here is what I learned. Medical researchers say breastfeeding is an *"irreplaceable* immunological resource" and should be placed at the top of global agendas because it is the primary source of active and passive immunity in the vulnerable early months and years of life. Milk, ingested from a mother's breast, is considered to be the most effective preventive means of reducing the death rate of children under five. [1] Antibodies in mothers' milk protect infants from illnesses like diarrhea and pneumonia. [2]

The medical community touts that breastfeeding our children is by far the best option and should always be our first choice. [3] The statistics are overwhelming. In an article titled "Breastfeeding Provides Irreplaceable Benefits For Babies," scientific research shows how consuming breast milk lowers your child's risk for sudden infant death syndrome, protects your child against infections and diabetes, and aids in the mother's recovery from labor, also lowering her risk of breast cancer. [4]

I finally understood what St. Teresa Benedicta, also known as Edith Stein, so beautifully said: "To be a mother is to nourish and protect true humanity and bring it to development." When I nestled Lillian in my arms, I felt the presence and love of God. Oh, how He must cherish me so to give me the gift of this precious child! What an honor to be her mother and to take seriously my irreplaceable role in feeding her.

The moment Lillian latched onto my breast, I just knew God was asking me to devote my body and life to nourishing her. My heart was wrecked with love for her. I reflected back on what Father Arnold described. I was sure now that God was inviting me to serve Him beautifully by mothering this baby. He had assigned me this beautiful soul to shepherd. God was inviting me to be fully available to mother her, and after just one glance at her, I could not resist. I was all in.

***

However, it wouldn't take long for reality to set in. Although I had read all the books and received advice from other mothers, I was not prepared for motherhood and the sacrifices it required. When I was discharged after labor and delivery, Lilli had to be admitted to the pediatrics floor for severe jaundice. I never left her side for days, quickly learning mothering was demanding and required a major shift in my priorities. I had to put someone else's needs above my own. And she had many. Motherhood required me to become more selfless. Caring for this baby consumed my energy and time, day and night. Still, I was drawn to this precious soul like a magnet. Lillian was my joy and delight. Nursing her, holding her, bathing her, and comforting her when she cried convinced me that God had given me this child for a purpose. She felt like a miracle.

But I had a confession. Mother Theresa said, "Love, to be real, must empty us of self," and motherhood emptied me of where I found my identity. As a new Mama, I often secretly felt my daughter's needs were an inconvenience to what I wanted to personally accomplish. Quite literally, having a baby put an eight-pound damper on my professional ambitions. I wrestled with God deeply over this. My husband and I were the first in our family and our large friend group to have children. Looking back, I was lonely and confused over my role as a mother. My television news job had given me a platform to share my gifts. When I stepped away from my career to raise our daughter, Lillian, I had many frustrating hours of feeling discontent and unseen.

When Lilli was old enough to sit in a high chair, she often "took" me out to lunch. Like, on the daily. I craved the energy of being around people taller than 36 inches, and eating a meal out broke up the monotony of our day at the farmhouse. I budgeted our weekly meal plan so that I had cash on hand for this treat. But one particular luncheon stands out because it radically changed the trajectory of my mothering. Forever.

I remember seeing this stylish, professional woman grabbing her meal from the counter and sliding into the booth next to where Lil and I were sitting. She was dressed beautifully in a black tailored suit (similar to what I had worn on television). Her nails were done (mine were hideous). She had on black wedges (last year's flip-flops for me). Her hair was pulled up, with curls around her face (when was the last time I washed my hair?) I remember watching her (yes, in a stalker-like way) and wishing for that day we could trade places. Maybe she was off after lunch to some important meeting where she was negotiating a commercial building lease or pitching a new sitcom. Perhaps she was a bank consultant or travel agent. The world was at her fingertips, and she didn't have a little munchkin on her hip holding her back. She looked sharp. And fresh. And I was sitting there alternating, spooning Broccoli Cheddar soup into my one-year-old's mouth and reminding her why she couldn't put ketchup on her baguette. I was hidden in the monotony of mothering while this other woman was out there changing the world.

I looked back at the woman and then at Lilli. I didn't feel like I had done anything academically productive for months. And I could feel my brain becoming mush. For those first six months after Lilli was born, I was convinced I had made the right decision to stop working and spend most of my hours mothering my baby. But now? I was losing steam. I felt left behind and uninteresting. It seemed like my gifts were melting into the mess of diapers and applesauce. Was all of my personal sacrifice worth it? That's when the woman (the one in the gorgeous, tailored suit) tapped me on the shoulder.

"Excuse me? Is this your daughter?" Lilli smiled and then spit out her soup. Chunks of chewed-up broccoli landed on my arm. Embarrassed, I looked everywhere for a napkin, but none was in sight. I nodded my head.

"She is stunning. Just adorable."

"Thank you," I muttered. Up close, she was even prettier than I thought. And did she have fake eyelashes? I leaned in closer. No, those lashes are actually hers, I think. She probably had time to put on her make-up, and she doesn't have bags under her eyes because she is most likely not chasing around kids all day. Especially dressed like that.

"Are you okay?" she asked me. Back to earth, Jodi.

"Oh yes, I'm sorry. I think it's my Mama-brain. Since I've had this child, I sometimes get distracted."

"Do you stay home with her?"

"Yes, I do." Lilli leaned over and kissed my shoulder. I pulled her from the high chair and onto my lap, sliding her soup bowl in front of me. She patted my face.

"I want to tell you something."

"You do?" Now Lil was digging in the soup with her hands. Those hands were so tiny. So perfect. I let her dig. I didn't even care. This woman already thought I was looney anyway. I might as well play the part.

"You are so blessed to be able to raise your own daughter. I was watching you while I ate my lunch. I have a daughter about that age, too."

"You were watching *us?*" I didn't even try to hide my surprise. The woman looked away. Her eyes brimmed over with tears.

"I am not as fortunate as you. My husband thinks I should work full-time, so we have an au pair. I barely see my daughter. And she doesn't feel comfortable with me the way I see your daughter with you. When my Ella comes home from being out with her provider, she doesn't even look for me. She'd rather have the nanny." I offered her a wadded-up napkin drenched in soup to dry the tears dripping down her face.

"Cherish this time with your girl. I know there are probably so many other things you could be doing. But you will never regret laying today's dreams aside to be with your kid. I do. I regret it every day. And I will never get that time back. I would trade the job, the money, all of it just to be the type of mother you are being."

For the rest of that day, I walked around with tears of gratitude in my eyes. When my husband came home from work, I ran up to him. I wrapped my arms around his neck, thanking him for prioritizing our family and working so hard so that I could stay home to raise our daughter. At bedtime, I prayed over Lillian and thanked God for this child.

That marked the day I started seeing my role as a mother as a privilege, not a penalty. I was beginning to see mothering as a freedom, not a punishment. God was inviting me to love, mold, and shepherd a soul.

Perhaps, my friend, you need that reminder today. Maybe you are knee-deep in the laundry or oh-so-tired of changing diapers. Perhaps you are discouraged with potty training, nap schedules, or constant whining. Maybe you are feeling restless and unfulfilled. You feel unseen. Lonely. I want to encourage you right now. You might feel stuck in the mundane, but do not be fooled for one second, Mama... you are doing no ordinary work. You, my friend, are doing kingdom work. The sacrifices you are personally making to mother your children are noble. There is no greater way to serve than steadily shepherding a little soul.

I love what Sally Clarkson says in *The Mission of Motherhood,* "I've come to appreciate the importance of the many thousands of routine moments in a mother's life, for it is in these moments that real greatness tends to be taught and caught. It is certainly important to grasp the great calling of motherhood and to respond to a vision of what a family can be. But it's the way I respond to my children in everyday moments that gives me the best chance of winning their hearts. If I have the integrity and patience in the small moments of life that are so important to my children, and if I approach them with a servant's heart, then I have a far better chance of influencing them in the larger and more critical issues of life." [5]

Do you view your role as a mother as a privilege, or does it feel more like a chore? It's okay to be dead honest. But I want you to be encouraged. You have answered a divine calling, the privilege of mothering your tribe. And it is not easy. But it is worth it.

Because I am prone to forget, I must remind myself daily how pivotal my role is in my children's lives. I also have to be mindful of the messaging I receive. One of the best ways I do this is to be purposeful in what social media I consume and who I "follow." Do their messages line up with God's calling on my life? Is what I am taking in encouraging me to embrace where God has me, not complain about it? Often, when I am distracted in my vocation of motherhood, I can reflect back and see that I have spent more time listening to the voices around me than listening to the voice of God. This is where my commitment to spending quiet time in His Scriptures has been life-changing. There, God reminds me of my purpose and His sovereignty. The Bible re-centers my heart and encourages me that my children are a gift.

Through mothering, God has shown me how much I need His strength to love my children. I can not do it without Him working through me. He continues to guide me to become less selfish, more patient, and, most of all - more reliant on Him. In serving my children, God has been drawing me into a deeper relationship with Him. It is a privilege to mother His children.

5

A Divided Heart

> *"To the world you may be one person; but to one person you may be the world."*
>
> Dr. Seuss

Five weeks after our second daughter was born, I pulled up in front of our local newspaper office boasting a laminated work name badge hanging from my jacket pocket and a breast pump tucked underneath my arm. I was giddy with excitement and exhausted from being up all night with a newborn. But no amount of sleep deprivation could squash my ambition. I had accepted a part-time writing gig at our local county newspaper. I was itching to do something outside of diapers, potty training, and dishes. The hours were flexible, the stories straightforward. This was a significant step down from my television gig. Still, I was okay with that because of the flexibility it provided. My beat was to cover the county commissioners and any big real estate development news. I would write features and filter in and out of school board meetings. The editor was kind and required very few office hours. I could write mostly from my desk at home. And I was eager to have a writing outlet. I dove into the juggling act of nursing a baby, raising a toddler, and managing our family time well so that I could produce quality stories for the newspaper. And I was still newly postpartum.

Whereas Lillian's birth had been a nightmare because I had "wisely" refused all drugs (years of talk therapy followed), Lacey's had been a dream. Again, my water would break in the middle of the night, almost two weeks before Lacey's due date, but enduring my first labor and delivery had made me wiser. My bag was packed, laundry was done, and after putting on an extra-large pad to soak up the water leaking down my legs, I returned to bed and slept soundly as my body began light contractions.

I also made another good decision for my personal health and recovery. I accepted an epidural, and it was purely magical. After the doctor handed me my newborn baby, Lacey immediately snuggled in, her brown eyes wide open and locked onto my face. For the first hour of her life, our second daughter did not cry. At all. At first, I panicked. Was this baby okay? Wasn't wailing a sign of a healthy life? I recall searching my husband's eyes for assurance that our beautiful girl was strong. He nodded his head and smiled. "Our girl is here, and she is doing just fine. She is so observant and serene and just wants to be close to you."

As I was holding my brown-eyed girl, I remember an older nurse coming to check on us and whispering in my ear, "Every baby is different. This one may be quieter than your first. Pull her closer to your face. She wants to be with her mother. She already knows your voice. Talk to her. Take her all in." Then, the nurse spoke words of wisdom that secured my role in my baby's life: *"God has assigned this precious soul to you, Jodi."* And I did as she told me. I pulled that beautiful baby close and inhaled all of her in. I can still smell my newborn Lacey Marie as I write this. This baby, this life was such a gift. Lacey would not take her eyes off of me. It was as if she was waiting to connect with me from the moment she was born.

My Lacey is almost sixteen now, and to this day, she remains calm and steady. Lacey gets me. She feels me. She senses my mood and wants to know what I am thinking. She always asks how she can help me. She is a servant. I just tucked her into bed tonight, and after tracing the sign of the cross on her forehead, she grabbed me around the neck and pulled me tight. "Are you doing okay tonight, Mama? How can I pray for you?" she asked. My husband says Lacey has my ability to minister to people, and she inherited my fierceness. That girl sure is tough. Lacey is a natural leader, not the bossy kind, but the type of leader others flock to follow. But I think Lacey's best gifts come from her father. She has my husband's intelligence and humble spirit. She is tender-hearted yet strong-willed. Lacey has the best laugh. She is magnetic because she is…herself. Loving this girl has changed me, and I can not even anticipate the incredible things the Lord will do with her one sacred life.

While baby Lacey was still nursing, I scheduled my part-time news writing hours around the girls' nap schedules. Once a week, my Mom would watch my daughters, and I would go into the newspaper office to work. But my babies were busy and full of energy. Although my Mama was fabulous with them, she was also tired. She had raised her kids decades ago and didn't have the energy to watch my girls for a full day. I would return from my reporting shift to needy children and a weary grandmother.

As the weeks flew by, working part-time for the newspaper, I found myself hustling to squeeze in more work hours during early mornings, nap times, and late nights so I would not have to ask my Mama to watch our girls. The Editor kept asking me to take on more assignments, and I obliged. As my newspaper workload grew, a tiny seed of irritation toward my children sprouted slowly and quietly into my heart. It was faint at first. It was so small that I barely recognized it. It wasn't something I was able to voice, but the more I said "yes" to the newspaper (and I loved it), the more I felt "inconvenienced" by the needs of my little ones. And let's face it. Two kids under the age of two are in a constant state of neediness. Simply stated, the "toddler" stage should be renamed instead to the "I-need-Mama's-full-attention" stage.

During this season, I was completely unprepared for the intensity of passionate devotion and connection I felt toward my children. My love for them was unlike anything I had ever felt, and I could sense how desperately they needed to be near me, how much they craved my presence and attention. But I had a writing job and deadlines to meet. I had difficulty reconciling my children's needs and my desire to work.

My heart was divided. I was split over how to best use my time. This dilemma felt eerily familiar. Again, I was at a stage where my professional work was fulfilling (and thriving), but I felt restlessness in my personal life. I decided that this part-time job was a huge blessing. If I was going to continue to pursue it, I needed consistent childcare for my children.

When my girls were two and four, I enrolled them part-time in a local childcare program. This was not an easy decision. I spent months searching out daycare homes until I found the woman I believed would be the best fit. Even with all of my research ahead of time, I literally had hives the first time I dropped the kids off. My brain was sending signals to my body that something was very off. I was unsettled and had a splintered heart.

The plan was that my young daughters would attend the daycare home twice a week. And guess what? It worked perfectly... for a few days. Lacey was an early and easy potty trainee who rarely had accidents. Lace wore big girl undies around the clock (even at night) and took great joy in her ability to go to the potty herself. Although I had discussed Lacey's toilet habits at length before we enrolled and was assured that even though Lace was the only child her age potty-trained, she would be guided to the toilet frequently, on the third day, I arrived to find my Lacey had wet her underwear. I was met by a frazzled and confused Lacey and a daycare owner who acted like she couldn't have cared less that my kid had peed her pants. Now, the daycare lady didn't mince words when she said to me bluntly, "I am a caregiver. Not your child's mother. I can't possibly pay attention to every detail of every child here, including yours." Strike One.

Strike Two was my (super social) Lilli begged me not to take her back there again. She said the kids were unkind, and one boy always stole her goldfish at snack time, and that when she needed help with the zipper on her jacket, she was ignored. But the primary reason Lilli didn't want to go back was that she longed for me. She told me she missed me praying before lunch and the books I always read to her when she climbed onto my lap before nap time. I had a pit in my stomach. I called a friend who had recommended the daycare home (her kids had been there years prior) and told her my concerns. She told me I needed to let the "small stuff" go and that these things were just part of putting my kids in part-time daycare. I listened to what she said and tried to swallow my uneasiness. But I knew deep down that the small stuff mattered to me because it mattered to my kids. The "small" stuff matters to a mother because she notices it all when it comes to her own child.

The final strike? It happened on just the fourth day of daycare. I arrived for pick-up and sat on the floor to help Lilli tie her shoes. Within minutes, I had two other children, who were not my own, climb onto my lap. They clung to me tightly, and I instinctively squeezed them back. These two lonely children were so desperate for their own mothers that they would take any stranger's lap just to feel loved. The one little girl looked up at me and, with wet eyes, begged, "Can you please call my Mama? I miss her. Why does she make me come here every day? I want to be with my mother." As the daycare provider peeled that child out of my arms, it literally broke my heart. After I loaded my kids into their car seats, I pulled our van to the side of the neighborhood street and heaved with tears. I looked in the rearview mirror at the two souls God had entrusted into my care, and I saw in the eyes of those small girls their deep desire to be fully seen and mothered. A substitute mother would not do. A daycare provider could not replace who they longed for most. They yearned for their mother.

That day, I scooped up my girls. We never returned. Not because it was an unfriendly, unsafe, or unclean place. The caregiver was kind and doing the best she could. I brought my children home that day because that is where they truly belonged - with me. I had something to offer them that no one else could: the safety and security of being their mother. I was irreplaceable.

Consulting the Holy Scriptures gave me personal confirmation of what God was asking me to do during this season in my life when my children were very young. In Luke 6:46, Jesus asks his disciples, "Why do you call me 'Lord, Lord' and not do what I tell you?" I felt God calling me to lay down my newspaper job for a season, but I resisted listening. My heart was divided and unsettled because I was not doing what God was personally asking me to do.

But there was more. God led me to a teaching in the gospel of Matthew that would rock my world and give me greater insight into why I felt so much division in my heart, showing me it was a universal struggle and not just something unique to my situation. I was unknowingly trying to serve two masters and failing at doing both.

In Matthew 6, Jesus' teaching is on fire as He addresses the topics of almsgiving, prayer, fasting, and storing up treasures and expands on the wisdom of having a sound eye. But when Jesus starts speaking in verse 24, He drops the hammer, at least for my heart when He says, "No one can serve two masters: for either he will hate the one and love the other, or he will be devoted to the one and despise the other. You can not serve God and mammon." (RSV)

Bible theologians explain that "mammon" is an Aramaic word meaning "wealth" or "property". They equate it to our earthly possessions or passions, the things we obsess over. [2] "Mammon" is what our heart treasures. This Scripture knocked my socks off. I was serving two masters, my devotion to one causing a dangerously small amount of resentment to sprout toward the other. On a deeper level, I was wrestling with the Lord of my life. Yes, I professed to know Jesus and wanted to follow Him. Still, I was most internally fixated on something else: doing what *I* wanted.

I learned that one of the biggest hindrances to loving God is prioritizing other things, namely my own desire, above Him. In my personal circumstance, I was placing my "need" to work (for personal fulfillment and some extra cash) above my call to motherhood. I loved God and wanted to follow Him, but I was obsessed with furthering my writing career. I was subconsciously finding my identity in working and staying relevant in the news business. Encountering Jesus' warning of serving two masters begged me to ask, "Is there something in my life that I am obeying or giving myself to more than my devotion to Jesus?"

As we grow in our knowledge of the Holy Scriptures and contemplate God's will in our personal lives, may we become wise enough to pause and ask, "Lord, what must I do? I want to be in love with you first. Please show me how to follow you and hear your call on my life. Show me the next step. Guide me in what action I can take to offer you my entire heart in this season of my life."

Perhaps you are reading this today, and your children are little, and you constantly battle the urge to leave your kids in the care of someone else during the day. Maybe it's because you feel ill-equipped or pressured by your spouse, or simply that when they are this little (and napping so much of the day anyway), it just doesn't really matter who they are with all day. Perhaps you've been told they will never remember this phase anyway, or you feel strapped for cash or inadequate and unsure of your mothering skills. I get it. I really do. Because for a spell, I wrestled with that too.

As mothers, it's easy to convince ourselves that someone could easily take our place. We hear the lie that there is someone out there with more patience, more grit, a softer tone, and more consistent discipline. We hear the lie that we are not that good at dealing with tiny babies or whiny toddlers or potty training and that someone else is better designed to nurture our children. We tell ourselves we are not "cut out" to be home and raise babies, and we should defer to someone who has more of a mothering skill set. The list can go on and on.

But let me whisper to you the truth that I felt deep in my gut and wished someone had the courage to counsel me all those years ago. When they are little, before they enter school, for the majority of the day...

Your kids need a Mother.
There simply is no substitute for you.

You, with your flaws and your short temper and your disorganization and your tendency toward discouragement or perfectionism or need for hyper-control. You and your crazy "requirement" for Starbucks coffee or Chick-fil-A drive-thru to survive. Your kid needs *you* as his mother. And when he's little, he needs *you* the majority of the time.

There is no replacement for long, uninterrupted hours spent with your child. This idea of quality time when they are toddlers is completely hogwash. Your boy needs quantity. For it's in the unplanned hours where the most opportunities to love and shepherd him are cultivated.

It is during the interruptions and unprompted conversations that you can best help mold your daughter's heart. Your son needs you, all of you. Your daughter needs the best part of you, present and engaged. There is no alternative for you.

Are you wrestling with your role as a mother? Are you constantly unsure how to spend your time or convinced you are not cut out to raise kids? I can relate. I felt that way too. In fact, I've met mothers from around our country, and they all feel the same way. We all share a common insecurity. Many of us silently wrestle with an unsettled heart. We all doubt our vocation in motherhood.

Remember, God has gifted you this holy privilege. Trust Him that He has made you a mother and will give you the grace to lean into that sacred vocation. Invite Jesus into your motherhood. Confide to Him your concerns. Talk to Him when you are insecure. Ask Jesus to fill in all the gaps where you feel incompetent. Isaiah 41:10, the Lord says, "Fear not, for I am with you; be not dismayed, for I am your God; I will strengthen you, I will help you, I will uphold you with my righteous right hand."

Take it to Jesus. Offer these questions to Him in prayer. Sit quietly with your concerns and offer your whole heart to the Lord. He will meet you there. And when He does, God will flood you with abundant reminders that He has gifted you this child on purpose.

6

Serving First Where I Am Most Irreplaceable

"This job has been given to me to do. Therefore, it is a gift. Therefore, it is a privilege. Therefore, it is an offering I may make to God. Therefore, it is to be done gladly if it is done for Him. Here, not somewhere else, I may learn God's way.
In this job, not in some other, God looks for faithfulness."

Elisabeth Elliot, Christian Missionary

During this mothering season, when I was tussling with God over how He was inviting me to mother my little girls, I sought the wisdom of a Christian counselor. I confided to her that I was so uncertain of what God was asking of me and shared my frustration. She was gracious, patient, and loving. But best of all, she asked questions that drew out the deep insecurities of my heart. My need for independence stemmed from a childhood wound. It was blocking my ability to surrender fully to the vocation of motherhood. As she helped me unravel the hurt places of my heart I had worked so hard to numb, I felt my divided heart start to heal. I began to believe my personal presence in my children's lives mattered.

As I sat on her couch, she showed me one specific diagram that forever is etched into my mind. My therapist pointed toward a picture of a baby just starting to crawl. If anyone knew a thing or two about babies, it was my counselor. Poised and professional, this beautiful woman had birthed and raised eleven kids. Yeah, you read that right. Eleven. Stinking. Kids. During our session, she gently walked me through the psychology of how a child best develops from an academic and spiritual perspective.

"And here is what we know to be true about human development," said Barbara Curano, licensed Catholic therapist. "Your security and self-esteem starts to be established just moments after you are born. A baby naturally cocks his head and looks up. When he first opens his eyes, he is searching for one thing. He desires to see the eyes of his mother. He desperately needs to know she is there. That she sees him. That she loves him." [2].

As I listened, my eyes began to well over thinking about all of the babies who will never get this gift of unconditional love and presence from their mothers. I shuddered thinking about the babies, who were just weeks new, looking intently for their Mother's smile, for her face to be watching theirs, and getting blank stares back instead. It is by God's divine design for a baby to see just far enough to find his mother. Your baby needs you. It is your gaze he longs to see. He wants to touch your face when he's happy. He reaches for your lap when he skins his knee or gets a boo-boo.

When my counselor explained this next part, I exhaled a huge prayer of gratitude that I had a fully present mother willing to give up many of her personal ambitions to pour her best energy and love into raising me.

"When a baby starts to crawl, he initially only goes as far away as he can see his mother," added Barbara. "Watch a baby do this. He moves and then pauses to look around. He turns a corner, but if he can't see his mother, he comes right back. He is always looking to see if she is watching. The baby wants to see if his mother sees him. That's how he determines that she cares. Her presence and her applause give him the confidence to keep going. Keep exploring. Keep growing.

But what's the most exciting part that we've learned about healthy emotional development? The baby isn't satisfied if someone notices. Even if someone "loving" is there, such as a friend, an aunt, or a grandparent...these people provide important relationships for a child later in life, but in the earliest years? The baby is always looking for one particular person to notice him and what he's accomplishing. He wants his mother to see." [3]

When your child is little, Mama, the only witness he cares about is *you*! He wants your attention when he pee-pees on the potty. He wants it to be your voice reading him books before naptime. You picking him up after he's fallen (yet again). You making his lunch sandwich, tucking him in at bedtime, and taking the time to sit to teach him how to tie his shoe. Your kid needs you. He needs his mother.

And it's tough to remember this when we see mamas plastered across social media feeds, TikTok reels, and anchoring cable news shows that say, "Of course, you can have it all. You can totally work 14-hour days, have three kids under four, and make your marriage work." But when you read between the lines, you see the brokenness behind the claims. One of my favorite female news anchors recently explained her tactic on how to prioritize her three small children yet balance working 60 hours a week, "I make sure I see them for at least 45 minutes each day. But it still breaks my heart how they all scream every time I leave for the day. They seem to never adjust to me not being around most of the time...They always prefer their mother."

Dear Mama, to raise healthy, confident, secure kids, let me tell you something that might be hard to swallow but gave me the courage to step wholeheartedly into making raising my kids my primary priority. When he is little, your kid needs you more than 45 minutes a day. And he's worth your time. Throughout his life, he will have a ton of schoolmates, excellent school teachers, loving family members, and Lord-willing grandparents and special friends. He will only ever have one mother. And that mother is you!

You are irreplaceable to your children.

Now let me pause here briefly to be crystal clear - your little one needs a healthy Mama, not an exhausted, frazzled one. And this is where we put the judgment card down and celebrate each other as mamas, acknowledging we all have different circumstances and need different outlets to help us mother at our best. We also have different financial constraints. What works best for me is probably not what will bless you. I'm not at all saying that we should not work some hours outside the home (because I sometimes do, and your income may be a necessity for your family!) or regularly hire a babysitter for date night (for those of you who still have littles, it is a glorious day when you stop paying a sitter and have your middle schooler do it instead!) or organize a lunch with girlfriends (yes, a lifesaver for me!) or let the littles stay at the grandparents every once in a while so we can have a overnight with our hubby (I just did this a few weeks back and it was so helpful!). Let's not take what I'm writing and get all black and white.

But what I am saying I think our generation of mothers really needs to hear. Because I needed to hear it. I was desperate to hear it. My divided heart and frustration were a warning flare that was an indicator of what my heart was believing. I was not sure I mattered as a mother. I now know I do.

The days are long with little ones at home, but the years are short. So when you have the choice, how are you prioritizing your kids? I encourage you to take inventory of your life right now. When you are at a crossroads, will you consider purposefully choosing to be physically present with your littles? Your choice has earthly and eternal consequences.

And here is where we get really practical. Choosing to be fully present where you matter the most requires constant sacrifice. Will you have to (often) say no sleeping in or fun nights out or bachelorette weekends away or no to work promotions or salary increases or picking up extra shifts to be physically and emotionally present with your child? Well, quite simply, yes. Like Winston Churchill said, "It often means choosing not what is best (for you), but what is required." Let's be honest here: it can feel frustrating to feel left out and left behind and like you're missing out on so much when you say a "no" for now to hang with your toddler.

But all the parties, the work accolades, and the weekends away have one thing in common. Those invitations are fickle. If you say no to one today, another one will be in your inbox tomorrow. Contrary to how it feels right now, you will have a chance to do all those things again. They will come back around. You'll get a second chance. Every *no* is a *yes* to something greater, a decision to make mothering your children one of your life's top priorities.

But your baby boy? Your little girl? That time when they hang on your every glance and light up when you clap and praise what they are doing? That time when they fall down and only want "Mama" to pick them up? That time is expiring. Your child will only be little for a little amount of time. There is no do-over for this sacred season of raising kids.

Do you feel like you are holding back part of yourself from your children? Are you constantly divided between your own desires and what your children really need from you? Perhaps today, God is inviting you to surrender your longing for more time away from your family inorder to pour your best effort into your children's lives. Can you ask God to help you give Him the parts of your heart you are holding back? Perhaps in letting go of the plans you hold so tightly, perhaps in offering pure surrender, you will find abundant peace.

"To fully experience our fulfillment in Christ and fulfill his will for our lives, we must come to the point where we give our whole selves to him - our freedom, our time, our bodies, all of our possessions and gifts- trusting him to show us how to use all that we are for his glory," writes Sally Clarkson. [4]

And with my heart pounding and tears rolling down my face as I type, let me assure you I have given up much to give my best energy and time to our kids. It has not been easy. I have turned down speaking engagements and opportunities to lead weekend retreats. I have said no to opportunities to write Bible Studies and emcee events. For a season when my four children were little, I prayerfully chose to say no to some incredible, awesome invitations for one purpose: to prioritize being physically and emotionally present to my children. But, as I witness our kids growing up and out (and yes, they are far from perfect!) and blossoming as teenagers as they grow in faith and stature, let me tell you that the choice I made to lean into the role where I was most irreplaceable, shepherding my children, has been worth every sacrifice. The time and energy I poured into loving them, delighting in them, correcting them, serving them, and embracing them when they were little have made parenting the middle and high school years a delight. I urge you to give your first and best energy to raising your children when they are little. It is a decision you will never regret.

7

The Assignment Desk

> *"Reflect upon what has been assigned to you."*
>
> Sirach 3:22

I worked the assignment desk when I first got my feet wet in the television news business. My post sat in the middle of the overcrowded newsroom, flanked by the cluttered desks of chatty reporters and a stone's throw away from our dingy editing booths. Our assignment lines would ring frequently with calls from local folks who thought they had the next big story to share. These sometimes centered around "breaking news" about a cat stuck for days up a neighborhood tree or a mother begging us to do a feature segment on her boy, insistent she was raising the next genius scientist, currently enrolled in kindergarten. I once spent over twenty minutes listening to a cranky man who wanted us to do a story on how his neighbor was violating his homeowners' association rules and close to an hour with a woman claiming she could predict the outcome of the next mayoral election by reading a set of playing cards. This is serious news, people.

As a reporter, I would collect and organize the story assignments. Still, I always breathed a sigh of relief that I was *not* responsible for the hardest part of the job: deciding which specific stories were assigned to which reporters. The actual "assignment" responsibility went to our news director on shift. Why? Because she knew the strengths and weaknesses of every reporter on her staff. She'd assessed our skills, knew how we worked under pressure and understood our temperaments. She was calculated in discerning which reporter would give the best attention to which story. But here's the part that surprised me most. Often, the news director did not appoint the news stories based on the reporter's merits. She carefully and thoughtfully assigned stories with one purpose: to help each reporter grow to his/her fullest potential. She matched reporters with specific assignments with intention. She wanted to cultivate their character.

Our Creator God does the same thing. God matches mothers with just the perfect and unique soul(s) to shepherd. He assigns us each child on purpose, for His purpose. God gifts us that particular child because He knows we are best wired to reach his heart. But that's not all. There's much more. God gifts us each individual child to grow *us*, to invite *us* to become molded more like Him.

In the same way, God used the mothers of those great men we read about in the last chapter to mold and form their hearts. God designed you with distinct gifts and passions that are unique to shepherding the heart of your child. You and your little one are not matched by accident. **God has assigned you that particular son or daughter on purpose.** He entrusted that specific soul to your care because He wired you with just what you need to reach the heart of that child.

Psalm 139:13-16 tells us that our child was "knit" and "woven together" by God in our womb. Our baby's "unformed body" was meticulously "fearfully and wonderfully" formed in a "secret place" by a Creator who designed all of her details before she even took her first breath. God placed that particular soul in your care so you could nourish her from conception through adulthood. Your son is a unique masterpiece of His creative genius.

Contrary to what popular culture tells us, a baby is not an accident that occurs when two people give their bodies and lives to each other. A baby is not a consequence. A baby is a heavenly post gifted by a sagacious giver. Motherhood is an invitation to grow in love, in relationship and dependence on Jesus Christ, and to direct a soul to find his or her rest in God.

The Holy Scriptures tell us that God created the first man and woman in the Garden of Eden, giving them their first joint "assignment." God instructed Eve and Adam to be open to having children. In Genesis 1, verse 28, God's first calling to Eve was to open her womb. He instructed the first couple to "be fruitful and multiply." And this was no ordinary "ask" for Eve. It was a holy assignment given to her by her Creator God.

The creation of the family was God's idea. The Bible says that children are a reward from Him! Because of this, God cares about how children are raised and nurtured. The Bible is clear that children are to be looked upon as a blessing, not an inconvenience. Proverbs 17:6 (NIV) tells us children are a treasure, "Children's children are a crown to the aged, and parents are the pride of their children."

But asking committed couples to be open to having children is so much more than an assignment. Asking spouses to be open to welcoming and shepherding children is a divine invitation. Sexual intimacy lures a husband and wife into a deeper relationship and passion with each other. But there is more! Our *yes*, our *fiat* to God's invitation to experience bliss in the marital bed, summons us into a deeper reliance on knowing and loving our Creator. It is an invitation to participate in love, in the life of God.

Author Sally Clarkson writes that God's design is not by accident, "Doesn't it make sense that a wise God who ordered the rest of creation in an intricate and systematic way, would also have provided such a person to care for children - to commit wholeheartedly to creating the right environment for them to grow and to prepare them to live throughout eternity bearing his image? I am convinced that God designed us as mothers to be that person in the lives of our children." [1]

As women, we have a choice to give our bodies and fertility to God within the marriage covenant. Because He is a gentleman, God does not require a husband and wife to do this. He invites us. He gives us free choice. The Roman Catholic Church teaches that sexual intimacy in marriage is intended for two purposes: to unify spouses and be open to creating new life. [2]

The pastoral constitution on the Church in the modern world, *Gaudium et Spes,* reaffirms that "marriage and conjugal love are by their nature ordered to the procreation and education of children" [3] and that the aim and meaning of conjugal life is to cooperate with the Creator in enlarging God's family. As cooperators with the Creator, we are "interpreters of his love ." [4]

I love how Catholic theologian Dr. Scott Hahn describes sexual intimacy as not just a physical act but a spiritual one, often resulting in the beautiful gift of creating new life, "God has designed the marital act to show the life-giving power of love. In the marital covenant, the two become one, and God has designed it so that when the two become one, they become so one that nine months later, you might just have to give it a name. And that child who is conceived embodies the oneness that God has made the two through the marital act. This is all the way that God has designed the marital covenant." [5]

Contrary to messages dominating our popular culture that some women are not cut out for motherhood, mothering children is nestled into our design. This call to mother is for all women. It is not exclusive to only those mothers who can bear children in their bellies. Danielle Bean, mother of eight, writes in her book *Momnipotent,* "We can understand our common call to motherhood as a womanly vocation to love, nurture, and care for the most needy among us. Those we care for might include biological children, adopted children, nieces, nephews, neighbors, students, patients, the disabled, the elderly, the poor, and any number of others in need of our love. Answering the womanly call to motherhood - to love- is a uniquely feminine privilege and responsibility." [6]

In her book *Discovering the Feminine Genius*, Katrina Zeno writes although every woman can not carry a baby in her womb, we all are called to spiritual motherhood because it is written into the very structure of a woman's being. "Women are created with the gift of interior readiness to receive others into their lives and, in doing so, to nurture their emotional, moral, cultural, and spiritual well-being. This is an exciting and creative challenge because women can be spiritual mothers anywhere: in the office, at home, and with their grandchildren, in the neighborhood, even sick in bed." [7]

God assigns children to our care because He has fashioned us with a nurturing heart. Although I didn't understand it during my early twenties, God taught me that He has set the call and desire to mother deep into my soul, deep in every woman's soul. Accepting God's holy invitation to become a mother radically transformed my heart. I did not understand how deeply my decision to be available first, where God was inviting me to serve, would impact my relationship with my husband and my understanding of God. But I do know one thing: answering a wholehearted *yes* to be the mother of the children God has assigned to my care has been worth it. Even in the messy moments, the exhaustion, and the seasons of doubt. Even in the grief of miscarriages and the sorrow of surrendering my womb to a hysterectomy. Accepting God's holy invitation to be a mother has entirely changed me. For the better. The restlessness I experienced as a new wife eventually evaporated when I surrendered my fertility to God. Our answer to God's invitation to become mothers summons us into a deeper reliance on knowing and loving our Creator. Parenting children is an invitation to cooperate in the life and love of God.

The children God assigns to my care will certainly not be the same ones He matches with you. Why? Because every human soul is unique.

God continually reminds me of this lesson, even as I mother kids approaching college age. I am writing on an airplane; our oldest daughter, Lilli, is sitting directly behind me. It's spring break, and we are heading to the sunshine state, ridiculously stoked to get away from the rigor of schoolwork, crazy sports schedules, and chores. It's time to lay on the shore and refresh. Lilli, just shy of her 17th birthday, had a travel volleyball tournament yesterday, so I stayed behind with her as my husband and three others headed down a day earlier. This morning, as we awaited to board our plane, Lilli and I searched for breakfast. But not just any food would do. Lilli is extremely limited in what she can eat.

Just after her first birthday, Lilli tagged along as I went about caring for my old bay quarter horse Buck, whom I adored. I couldn't wait to teach Lilli to ride and dreamed of one day getting her a pony so we could explore the local riding trails together. I positioned Lilli a few feet shy of where I tacked up my horse in a playpen with a few toys when I noticed her clawing at her skin. I ran over and scooped her up to find she was covered in red, blotchy hives. Within minutes, my little girl's eyes started to swell shut. I ran to our house and put her into the shower. It was the first time I had experienced seeing a toddler have an anaphylactic reaction, and it was terrifying. Lilli recovered a few hours later, but extensive blood work and a bland diet were ordered as the allergy experts tried to assess what had caused such a severe response. I remember Lilli was sitting in the high chair in our farmhouse kitchen, her tray covered in little green peas and Cheerios, when the doctor called with the results. I had to sit down to comprehend what he was saying.

"I've been doing this a long time, and I know your husband's family has a history of food allergies, but I've rarely seen allergy markers so high in so many categories," our trusted pediatrician told me. And then he rattled off the list: wheat, egg, milk, beef. Tree-nuts. Apples. Peaches. Pears. She was even allergic to some vegetables, like peas! I looked over to see Lilli putting a pea into her mouth. I quickly slammed down the phone, swiped the little mushed green balls from Lilli's tray, and threw them into the trash can. "But doctor, I'm feeding her peas right now! Are you kidding me?" I heard him sigh. He wasn't done. "The most concerning part, Jodi, is I'm afraid she has an adult type 5 (the highest marker) allergy to horses. Exposure to horses can cause a serious anaphylactic reaction. I'm afraid you will have to radically change what foods you offer Lilli and the activities you do with her." To say I was stunned was an understatement. I looked out at the pasture, where my horse was grazing, as I experienced a wave of total shock.

Although I was thankful the blood work had uncovered the mystery of Lilli's hives, the next few months would prove to be incredibly difficult as we muddled through how to feed this child. And here is where I get really, really transparent. Cooking and food prep are not my jam. Give me loads of dirty laundry and a messy bathroom; I'm your gal. Assign me a closet to organize or a room to decorate, and I'll do it with a smile, with HGTV bravo. Need your yard mulched? Girl, I got ya. I'll tackle those jobs without a lick of complaining while humming a Dolly Parton tune. But meal planning, grocery shopping, refrigerator organization, and baking? While I don't have the blood work to prove it, let's just say anything that requires me to work for too many hours in the kitchen gives *me* hives. While I tried my best, and still do, I get overwhelmed easily in this area. It's just not my strong suit. There, I said it. I tell people I'm sure God would have gifted us over a dozen kids if those little ones didn't have the audacity to require three meals a day (plus snacks).

So you can imagine how astonished I was to discover God gave me a daughter who needed a very specialized diet, lots of food preparation, and detailed meal planning. The surprise "cherry" on top? Not only would I have to give up my dream of riding horses off into the sunset with Lilli, but I would also have to take painstaking measures to sanitize myself and take off anything that might have horse dander on it before I could be around my daughter. I remember asking God, "Surely this is a joke!" One afternoon, feeling frightened and frustrated and out of ideas on what to feed her, I hit my knees sobbing, confiding to the Lord in prayer that I felt so ill-equipped to mother the needs of the child He had given me.

I learned, and am still gleaning today, that God did not accidentally assign Lilli to my care. In His wisdom, God gifted her to me so that He might work through my weaknesses, not despite them. The number of hours we have logged researching good food options, the thousands of lunches I have packed to ensure Lilli has enough to eat when she is out, the deep belly laughs we have had when recipes I attempted came out disgusting (some labeled "inedible") have created a ridiculous closeness between me and my oldest girl. She has told me time and time again how much she appreciates the effort I put into her food prep and has let me know how loved she feels. She trusts that I want what is best for her. Now that she is older, she recognizes and expresses gratitude for my sacrifice. She hugs me fiercely when I trek to a far-off bakery to load up on her favorite gluten-free muffins. "My love language must be gifts of food," Lilli told me recently as she winked one of those gorgeous blue eyes. I winked back. I've been the main one there to comfort her, to hold her hand during specialist appointments, to make her laugh, and to witness her journey. A mother's love is a beautiful thing to behold. God's Word often compares a mother's love for her child to His love for His people because it is unwavering. Take Isaiah 66:13, for example,

"As a mother comforts her child, so will I comfort you; and you will be comforted over Jerusalem."

Lilli scarfed down her breakfast this morning at the airport and smiled wide at me. "I know this is the first time we have traveled separately from the rest of the family, but I was just telling a friend of mine how I was looking forward to traveling alone with you, Mom. We have the best time together, and I love being with you." I smile wide. Thank God He is the assignment editor, not me. 1 Corinthians 7:17 says, "Only, let every one lead the life which the Lord has *assigned* to him, and in which God has *called* him." I am grateful God assigned Lilli to me, and I have matured greatly from caring for her. And I share this next part of my mothering story with a huge smile on my face. Because it is a testimony of God's kindness and beautiful mercy toward me.

God, in only the tender way He can, is well aware of my weak spots, but He also gifted me my youngest daughter, who lights up when she enters the kitchen instead of shrinking back. Annabelle has an infectious passion for cooking and baking and will take on any recipe. She delights in whipping up new desserts for Lilli. She has inspired me to purchase hard-to-pronounce ingredients and navigate cookbooks with enthusiasm. Annabelle's enthusiasm for wearing an apron has balanced out my insecurity in the kitchen, nudging me to grow and become more comfortable in the area where I have felt the weakest. God certainly does not assign us our children by accident. He knows just who we need. Praise be to Him and all of His infinite wisdom.

God's appointments in motherhood will look differently for every woman. How are you doing today with accepting yours? We have the assignment of loving each soul God has gifted us, providing protection for them, shepherding their hearts, and then prayerfully releasing them into the service of God.

Let's put our judgment cards down and trust that God has specific callings on our motherhood. Let's celebrate our feminine designs, not compare them. Let's champion each other in our mothering vocations, not compete about who has the most car seats installed in their vehicle. Let's ask for the maturity to keep our eyes focused on our Lord and how He's inviting us to be personally available for His invitation to motherhood. And when God assigns each of us a unique and beautiful soul to mother, let's throw our arms and hearts open wide to His invitation to love, knowing that He has matched us on purpose, asking God to guide and equip us.

8

You Blinded Me
With Science

"The reality is that motherhood is hardwired into a woman's soul, whether she is conscious of it or not."

Carrie Gress

We sat on metal stools flanked across my kitchen island, her ten-month-old asleep in her arms, as we politely shuffled through light conversation. We talked about the weather and the trail that had just been paved down our island road. We discussed the neighbor who was spending what felt like months rehabbing his house. But I could tell something else was more pressing on her mind. After a few awkward moments, she shifted her weight on the stool, looked down at her empty tea cup, and said quietly, *"I need to get your opinion on something, but first let me say, I'm not religious like you, Jodi. I appreciate and respect your faith and how you are raising your kids, but I will make my decision on what education and sociologists say is best for my kid, not what some God might think I should do."* I nodded my head, encouraging her to share more. The two of us had a unique friendship, although she was ten years younger. She was there for me when my kids were little, and knew I was witnessing her raising her own. Although we adhered to vastly different life ideologies, our relationship had been founded on authenticity. During this moment, I appreciated her honesty.

For the next hour, my young friend unloaded her struggle over whether to return to her demanding job or make arrangements to cut back her hours to be home more with her first baby. Her deciding factor on what to do with her little one boiled down to one measure: her daughter's future self-esteem. She wanted to know which choice would help her child grow to become a confident, healthy, and mature adult. And then she said it, and I felt the chills cascade up my arms, *"Jodi, you seem to make your parenting decisions based on spirituality. Mine will be based on science."* I smiled big and poured her another cup of tea because she had unknowingly thrown me a softball. I knew the scientific evidence that a mother's influence on the early years of life would be a home run.

Over the recent years, as I speak to women around the country, I have noted a striking trend among young mothers today. It appears to me that even among professing Christian mothers, explaining God's principles of motherhood (as I will expound on in Part II) is not enough to convince mothers to make purposeful decisions to become the primary daily caregivers of their little ones. They need more. They need spiritual truths supported by science. And I get that. Because as a journalist and a woman, I needed that too.

The questions that circle mothers' hearts have a central theme: *"Will my kid be happy? What can I do to guarantee my daughter will feel loved? How can I best teach him to become a contributing member to society and be a good friend/spouse?"*

Over the past decade, I've combed over numerous medical journals, scientific studies, neurobiological research, news articles, records of psychoanalysts, and observational essays from pediatricians- anything I could get my hands on to see what the academic, medical, and social fields have to say about the impact motherhood has on a child. The science is blinding. It's not just God and the Catholic Church who tout the benefits of a mother's irreplaceable role in her child's life. Even if a mother is opposed to religious faith formation or a flat-out atheist, if she desires to raise a healthy, secure, confident child (I have yet to meet a mother who does not want this for their son or daughter), the collective science makes a serious, consistent, and compelling argument that a mother's commitment and physical presence during her child's early years make a distinct mark on the outcome of her child's life. Science says a mother's decision to pour her best energy, time, and affection into being the primary caregiver of her young child matters, both when he is little and when he grows into an adult.

In her book *Being There: Why Prioritizing Motherhood in the First Three Years Matters,* psychoanalyst Erica Komisar argues that society needs to understand and respect the unique and essential place a mother has in her child's life, especially in the first three years. [2] Komisar has the credentials to back her findings up. Based on more than two decades of clinical work, established psychoanalytic theory, and studying the most cutting-edge neurobiological research on caregiving, attachment, and brain development, Komisar has found "indisputable" research that the years before age three in a child's life present a "crucial, formative window." [3]

Former President of the American Academy of Pediatrics, Dr. Thomas K. McInerny, agrees, citing that the nurturing presence of a mother in her child's early years even affects the development of her child's brain. "Frequent positive interaction between a mother and a baby in the first three years of life is crucially important for the child's social and cognitive development." [4] A study released by the Stanford University School of Medicine shows scientific proof that a child's brain responds more strongly to her mother's voice than the voices of strangers. It concludes that the brain regions engaged when a mother interacts with her child are not just with auditory processing but also with emotional and social functions. [5]

Women now spend 50 percent less time with their children than mothers did five decades ago. [6] The statistics of American children's overall health, even before the COVID pandemic hit, are sobering. The *National Review* reported, "By every available measure, including school achievement and the incidence of delinquency, depression, sexual promiscuity, suicide, and substance abuse, the well-being of American children has declined in recent decades." [7] Komisar and others like her treat children and adults for problems related to early relationship loss and trauma, including behavioral and developmental issues. She said her clinical research has pointed to one common thread that can be traced to early childhood, "From my firsthand professional observations, I have come to understand the connections between these symptoms and disorders and the emotional and physical absence of young children's mothers in their day-to-day lives." [8]

Komisar believes our society is overlooking a growing body of scientific evidence, including neuroscience and hormonal, attachment, and epigenetic research, that supports how critical it is for a mother to be the chief caregiver of her child during the early formative years by being both emotionally and physically present. [9]

So often, mothers put their work and needs ahead of their children's. The result has long-term consequences. [10] Komisar said an increasing number of parents are coming to see her because they are concerned that their children are suffering with depression, eating disorders, aggression, anxiety, and addictions (issues clinical data confirms are all on the rise today). These parents are baffled as to why their children are struggling. Still, to Komisar, who treats these patients, the evidence points in one direction. "It's clear to me that these symptoms are often related to the premature separation of children from their mothers. These are women who, despite their best intentions, and whether they stay at home or work outside the home, may not know how to be present for their child or how to recognize the signs that their child is in distress." [11]

Economist James Tooley hardly finds it to be a coincidence that there is a sharp decline in the happiness/security of children and an up-tick in women allocating their best energy and time *outside* of their families, "We've swapped a society where women could be full-time mothers - a role many found fulfilling and satisfying - for one that fuels consumerism and clogs our roads with second cars on the drive to school, where spoiled children, buried under mountains of toys they can't be bothered to play with, watch suggestive TV shows in their lonely bedrooms. And we have this partly too because the equality feminists force us to believe that motherhood was parasitic, the housewife a leech." [12]

Our decisions as mothers and how we prioritize our time spent with our child(ren) will directly impact their future security, success, and overall happiness. I have seen this in the lives of my own children, especially as we prepare to launch our oldest out of high school and into the adult world.

We currently board our horses at the property of a retired horse breeder who lives just up the road from our farmhouse. This requires us to trek down our quiet island road twice daily to care for our animals. Although horseback riding is my daughter Lacey's primary passion, caring for our horses often is a family affair. Our oldest, Lilli, sometimes plays chauffeur, shuttling her sister to and from the horse property. Annabelle and Tripp help groom the horses, move hay bales, and muck out yucky stalls. All of the kids have learned to help serve their sister (and often have to be reminded to not complain).

The owner of the barn stopped me yesterday, saying he needed to chat with me about something. I held my breath, waiting for a reprimand. Surely, we had forgotten to turn off a running water bib or neglected to sweep the aisle of horse debris. I wondered if perhaps he had overheard my frustrating mothering session earlier that week when I had to correct my son for irritating his sister (I think he may have "accidentally" thrown a pitch-fork of manure at her face, but the two sides involved couldn't agree on what actually happened when I quizzed them so it felt like holding a mock-trial to get the scoop. Shocker, my son was guilty.)

I rolled my shoulders back, steeling myself for some sort of parenting chastisement from this older, wiser man. Instead, he put his hand on my shoulder.

"I've had a lot of kids and families come in and out of here over the last few decades. Teenagers of all kinds have been at our barns, and I have seen parenting of all different types."

He paused.

"Jodi, I mean this with all sincerity. I do not know how or what you are doing to raise this crew of yours, but keep it up. I have never encountered kids with such exceptional manners, ones who look me in the eye to greet me each time I come around. Your kids take correction from me without making excuses. They seem to have good self-esteem.

But mostly, I see how much you delight in each of them and how much respect they feel for you."

My eyes could not help but glisten over. I was sweaty and covered in horse stall pine shavings, but I threw my arms around this man and hugged him tightly anyway. His words spoke much-needed encouragement into my heart. That very day, I had been doubting my mothering vocation, and I needed the reminder that my commitment to raising my kids with intention was making a difference. Our barn manager gave me something we mothers are often lacking: an outside perspective. When I can sometimes get discouraged by all of the frustrating behavior of my little crew and my insecurity in parenting, he was witnessing the fruit blooming in the lives of my children and was kind enough to voice it.

How often, as mothers, do we get stuck with tunnel vision tending to the "weeds" we see sprouting in our children's hearts (annoyances or bad behaviors) that we forget to pause, step back, and acknowledge the beauty that is also slowly growing inside of them?

Our barn manager doesn't have a medical degree, but he is a witness to what medical experts observing child development, such as Komisar, conclude, "Spending more time with your child during this critical period of development means she will have a greater chance of being emotionally secure and resilient to stress as well as being better able to regulate her emotions throughout life, read others' social cues, achieve a higher emotional intelligence, and connect with others intimately," [13]

Put quite simply- as I told my young friend over tea that afternoon in my kitchen, the medical science and social research regarding a mother's impact on her child's life is quite compelling. Our commitment to spend significant time mothering our child daily makes a monumental difference in his life. None of us will parent perfectly, but our decision to give our best energy, time, care, and affection to our child will have lasting repercussions on him for the rest of his life. As a mother, you have an irreplaceable role in molding your child. The science is blinding.

PART II:

THE PRINCIPLES
LIVING OUT YOUR CALLING

PRINCIPLE [prin-*ci-ple*] -*noun*

1. a fundamental truth or proposition that serves as the foundation for a system of belief or chain of behaviors (See also: 'truth,' 'philosophy', 'thesis'.)

9

The Ambassador

"This must be some kinda sick joke," I remember saying to my husband as I wailed in grimacing pain. I was clutching the rails of the sterile bathroom, with amniotic fluid dripping down my legs. Our little guy was over a week past his due date, and I had arrived at the hospital earlier that day to be induced. The contractions had come and gone all day, but the Pitocin drip had rendered little effect on my cervix (sorry for sharing the specifics, but as one of my girlfriends begged me recently, "Jodi, please don't spare the messy details when you write. We all want to know them anyway!" Sorry, Dad.) All day during the induction, I was relaxed and doing just "peachy keen" in pure heaven because my hubby and I could watch cable TV all alone without the interruptions of tiny ones. That is until the doc reached his arm up my you-know-what to check the baby, surprising me by pulling out a big old needle to break my bag of water. Within four minutes, I went from smiling to complete agony and full-on-stinking labor. I begged the doctor for an epidural. Yes, going from a pain level of one to ten in a matter of minutes was insane, but the craziest part? I would deliver our little boy in pitch black under the rays of a portable spotlight. You read that right. Yeah, by now, you kinda know me; I just can't make this stuff up.

Here's how it all went down. When we checked into the hospital earlier that morning, we were greeted with a warning that the facility would undergo its first-ever "scheduled" power outage later that evening. The hospital wanted to check its emergency functions in case of a catastrophe and ensure all of its employees knew how to follow protocol if there was a power failure (yes, ironic, because the hospital is precisely where people head when there is a catastrophe). So we were briefed that the hospital would officially go off the grid that evening from sundown to sun-up. Of course, the triage nurse told me none of this would affect my laboring because I would surely have this baby out by noon. Uh-huh. Sure.

Not only was he not out by noon, but my baby boy was still not budging by nightfall, as the hospital deliberately shut down the power. My hospital room was enveloped in darkness and would have been peaceful if I was on a silent, spiritual retreat. But I was in labor. After the doctor broke my water, things got chaotic. Quick. Oh, and in the pitch black.

In the nick of time, I did get the epidural, as the nurse held up a flashlight so the anesthesiologist could see where to poke his magical medicine into my back. And there is nothing to make a woman in labor feel more relaxed and attractive, like rolling in a giant spotlight and aiming it at her unmentionables while she frantically tells the doctor the baby is crowning. There would have been more light, and I would have been able to see better if I were delivering in a movie theater. At least there would have been buttered popcorn and Twizzlers to keep me motivated. As the doctor instructed me to push, I remember feeling around to squeeze my husband's hand because I couldn't see his face. Because I was delivering in a blackout. So help me God.

After just a few pushes, we met our little guy, David, at 10:10 pm. We were in awe when we met our son, whom we nicknamed Tripp, because he is the third in a line of David's and our third kid. He was our biggest baby yet, a healthy nine pounds with piercing blue eyes. He was pink as could be and strong as an ox from the day he was born.

One of the most sacred memories of my entire life is when our girls got to climb onto our hospital bed and meet their baby brother for the first time. If I close my eyes, I can still feel that moment. The preciousness of new life and the deep love between our family. It was one of the most beautiful moments of my life.

I remember laying him on my breast during the quiet of the night and being overcome with such emotion it is dripping down my face right now, even as I write this. I thanked God for the gift of a son who would carry on my husband's name. I whispered low to my boy and prayed over him, "God bless you, my child. We have prayed for you, and God has been faithful. You are named after your father and his father. And you are named after the greatest King who has lived. The only King who the Scriptures say had a heart like God. May you be a warrior like your father. And may you be humble like King David."

The weeks and months after David came home are some of the most sacred of my life. It began a season where I learned to create practical rhythms for our growing family and finally fully embrace living out my calling to motherhood. Shepherding three little ones under the age of four was busy. Lacey was already potty-trained, so she and Lilli helped me change diapers and bathe their little brother. They pushed David around in their baby-doll stroller (not super safe, I guess, but crazy cute, and of course, I was monitoring their every move). I worked hard to get all three of my "babies" on the same nap schedule, so I had the much-needed quiet time each afternoon to myself. We played dress-up and danced around the living room, made forts, and constructed hours of pretend food out of Play-Doh.

I poured my entire heart into Lilli, Lacey, and David and experienced a calmness in my soul like never before. After David's birth and my decision to step down from working for the newspaper, I gave the breast pump away. I nursed him organically without the stress of bottles and saving up milk. There was such a freedom in not trying to do it all. God invited me to be fully present to my children. My new mantra became a quote I scribbled across the front of my journal by missionary Jim Elliot, "Wherever you are, be all there."

In this season of my life, I knew that God was calling me to give my all to these little ones. And they required a lot. A whole lot. If you've tried grocery shopping with a three-month-old, two-year-old, and four-year-old, you certainly understand! We, mamas, aren't insane (even though I remember one older man calling me that when I was in aisle eight at Whole Foods). Mothers are flat-out superheroes (and hungry from breastfeeding and managing a lot of tiny people.)

David continued to grow strong. At just ten days old (I have the video to prove it), that little turkey rolled himself totally over. I jokingly told my husband we should have named him Samson. He was utterly smitten with his older sisters, always trying to keep up. I remember a few days after he was born; it was a glorious late-October day, and I took the kids on a walk. David was tucked into the stroller, Lacey was walking, squeezing my hand, and Lilli was riding her bike alongside. I stopped to look at the captivating blue sky and felt God's love engulfing me and my children. I was completely where God was asking me to be, and the joy that radiated from that decision to have children was unlike anything I had ever experienced in this life and certainly not when I was on television. My worldly ambition was waning, replaced by my desire to mother; my call to serve first was where I was most irreplaceable. Motherhood began to fill me up. When someone asked what I did, I started to confidently respond, "I am a mother!" My identity shifted during those months. I no longer was fixated and obsessed with my career. Instead, I was finding my purpose in the mission of raising these three children. And I loved it.

My boy turned twelve last month. He is growing up in so many ways, but mostly in his knowledge and love of our Lord. He is full of life. And passion. And still so very strong. He is gifted athletically and a favorite among the kids at school. Mothering a son has stretched me. It has also made me more tender. This boy has my entire heart. I love him so much it hurts.

Tonight, he and I played basketball in the pole barn as the sun was setting. Afterward, he ran into my arms, and I scooped that sweaty boy up and squeezed him so tight. He is testing the world now. Trying to find his way among the other boys, sometimes pushing against what we teach him. And in those moments, I am grateful because it means he is becoming independent and thinking for himself. He's also crazy obsessed with his Daddy. Mothering him in this season has meant letting him lean toward his earthly father when he has always preferred me. It is hard to let go, but so beautiful too.

Motherhood stretches us. Constantly. Mothering never allows our hearts to stay still or stagnant. It calls us into a deeper relationship with Jesus and trusting Him with our sons and daughters. Motherhood invites us, as Holocaust survivor Corrie Ten Boom so famously said, "To hold all things loosely." It gives a reason to celebrate each season of letting go. This never gets easier. Just ask the mama who dropped her girl at college or watched her son waiting at the altar for his bride to walk up the aisle. Talk to the woman learning to give her daughter-in-law the freedom to mother differently than she did or show grace when her adult son's decision to abandon a good-paying job to start a non-profit makes her chest tighten. Choosing a new life is opening ourselves up to love. It truly is like watching our heart walk along the outside of our chest.

Being a mother is a holy responsibility. Motherhood is a sacred privilege and a ministry with heavenly consequences. At the end of our lives, we will have to give an account to God on how seriously we prioritized the tender souls He has assigned to our charge. 2 Timothy 2:15 says, "Do your best to present yourself to God as one approved, a workman who has no need to be ashamed, rightly handling the word of truth." We will have to answer to God the Father in how we raise the children He entrusted to our care.

One of the core principles of motherhood begins with the radical truth that our children do not actually belong to us. Psalms 127:3 tells us that our children are God's possession, made for His purpose. Every child God gives to us truly belongs to Him first.

So how does God ask us to mother the children He has personally assigned to us? How can we be good disciples in motherhood? Author Paul David Tripp answers this question in his excellent book *Parenting*. Jesus asks us to be His *ambassadors*. In 2 Corinthians 5:20, St. Paul tells us, "We are ambassadors for Christ, as if God were appealing through us." This is something we must practice over and over.

The Latin root word for Ambassador is AMBACTUS. It means "vessel, servant". An ambassador is a person sent on a mission to represent another. She is an apostle, an evangelist, a missionary, a messenger, a mouthpiece, a spokesperson, and a courier (and I have the mileage on my black mini-van to prove it!). **An ambassador mother's job is to faithfully represent the message, methods, and the character of the leader who has sent her.** [2]

It is so humbling for me to admit that living as an ambassador mother goes against every natural fiber in my body! Why? Because I love to be in control, and it can be tempting to fall into the trap of thinking, "Well, these are *my* children and I can parent them as I see fit! I get to decide how to raise them!" But an ambassador mother doesn't see her child as *her* trophy, but a trophy of the risen Savior who she seeks to serve! [3]

As mothers, we have one chief goal in mind: to raise our children to fall deeply in love with Jesus Christ so that His love will transform their lives. When we view our children as gifts rather than possessions, we can disciple our tribe with a deep sense of purpose and meaning.

As mothers, we are in holy warfare. The fight? It is over the salvation of our children. Do you know the enemy is working double-time to strip you of your joy in mothering because he wants to distract you from your vocation of reaching your child's soul for Jesus? As Catholic theologian Peter Kreeft says, "This (spiritual) war begins and ends at (our) back door." [4] (Much more on this in Part III).

My dear friend and bridesmaid, Becky, travels the world as a United States Ambassador. She spent years preparing to be a representative of our country. This job is quite an honor, but she had to first be diligent in studying the ins and outs of one monumental thing. Becky had to know the U.S. Constitution from front to back to be a confident communicator representing the values of the United States. As Christian mothers, we need to know where our Heavenly Father stands so we can consistently convey His truths to our children. We need to be saturated in His Word, the Bible, to serve as God's ambassadors.

2 Timothy 3:16-17 says, "All Scripture is inspired by God and profitable for teaching, for reproof, for correction, and for training in righteousness, that the man of God may be complete for every good work."

To train our children's hearts, we have to be purposeful in first training our own. We can not teach what we do not know. The mothers of great men, such as our nation's founding fathers, knew how to reach their children's hearts. Author Ginger Plowman writes, "They knew the importance of God's Word in training and nurturing their little boys. They understood biblical discipline and they faithfully instructed their children in the ways of the Lord." [5]

An ambassador mother acts on behalf of the one who has sent her. This means we model and then teach our children God's standards, not the standard of popular culture. A mother who is a disciple of Jesus Christ believes her life is under His authority, and it is her job to model this to her children. When we see ourselves as representatives of someone greater, wiser, more powerful, and more loving than us, we can exhale, believing our daily work is not to turn our children into what the world says is important but to turn them to Jesus Christ. We see our mothering as an instrument in the hands of God, who wants us to communicate His power to rescue and transform our children's lives.

Catholic Saint and physician Gianna Molla understood this well. Diagnosed with terminal cancer during her fifth pregnancy, St. Gianna told doctors she was willing to give her life if needed to spare her child. Although the baby arrived safely, this beautiful and sacrificial mother was suffering from severe abdominal pain. She would tragically die just seven days after her daughter was born. Saint Gianna believed her primary mission was to serve as an ambassador of Jesus Christ saying, "We must be living witnesses of the Beauty and Grandeur of Christianity."

When we believe as mothers that we have been appointed by the heavenly King, it is crucial to remember that our children's journey to discovering a personal relationship with God will be much different than our personal stories. It can be tempting to take our children's mistakes and choices to sin personally. It can painfully feel like their missteps are made directly against *us*. But in those moments, we have an opportunity to stand alongside our children and point them back to their need for our Savior.

How do we put this into practice in real life? When our children mess up or make a wrong decision, we can pivot from saying, "How could you do this to me?" to softly, "Honey, this violates who God has called you to be."

Just yesterday, I found myself in a position where Jesus asked me to intervene on His behalf to reach my child's heart. We were out to lunch after Mass when our youngest was insistent on whining. About everything.. If there was an Olympic competition for "loudest first-grade fusser," she would have taken home the gold. Like, this was epic, people. I quietly asked her to stop several times and show some self-control over her words. Still, she loudly disobeyed, throwing a crying fit. As we waited for our food, what should have been an enjoyable meal (giving me a much-needed break from cooking) and lively family conversation around the table turned into a miserable experience for our entire family as Annabelle insisted on getting her way. She wanted lemonade instead of water. A burger instead of "disgusting" chicken. And she complained that it was "horrible" that we had to go out to eat. Yes, we actually "torture" our children by taking them out to lunch. Can I get a witness?

And honestly, I was tired. I was tempted to just ignore her poor behavior and enjoy my sweet tea, but God nudged me to get up and take Annabelle outside to address her behavior. God loved Annabelle enough to ask me to shepherd her wayward heart.

When I am correcting one of our children, I often say, "I love you so much and it hurts God's heart that you are disobeying. I am disciplining you because God has asked Mama to teach you His ways. I am accountable to our Lord for how I mother you. And God says this behavior is a no!" Fifteen minutes later, after Annabelle received her consequence, we returned to the lunch table with smiles, ready for her to try again, this time minus the whining.

As an ambassador, the goal of mothering is not to control our children's behavior but rather to reach their hearts for Jesus Christ. Following this principle often requires selfless and tireless work. But God loves us and our children enough to not let us stay as we are. He longs to transform us into His image.

10

Available

When our daughter Lacey was nine, she had a tough year. An injured ankle kept her sidelined through soccer and basketball seasons, and she felt left out and left behind. A natural introvert, or so I thought until she entered middle school and became Miss Popular, we saw our middle daughter slip into herself and sort of disappear socially, a scary thing to witness. But Lacey had one constant joy: her love of animals. Years ago, we adopted a white goldendoodle named Biscuit, and he was glued to Lacey's side as her ankle healed. Lacey dreamed of raising puppies and poured all of her free time into reading, researching, and scheming on how to get a female dog and start her puppy breeding business.

For her 10th birthday, our family surprised Lacey with a scavenger hunt of clues, leading us on a day trip across Maryland. We took Polaroid snapshots at each stop, ending at our final surprise destination - a goldendoodle breeder where Lacey would select her new female puppy. Lacey was on cloud nine, choosing an apricot pup with a big white patch on her chest and white paws. She named her Sunny. After a rough season of struggle, we watched our little girl light up as she tenderly raised Sunny. As the puppy grew, so did Lacey's attachment to her. Lacey did chores to raise money to buy supplies for her puppy business. Sunny was just months away from being old enough to have puppies, and it was all Lacey talked about. When she went to school, Lacey would leave me detailed notes (addressed to "Sunny's Grandmother") on how to care for her beloved pup when she was away. Lace would rush home and spend her entire time until bedtime with her dog.

And then an unthinkable accident happened. Unbeknownst to my husband, Sunny climbed under his vehicle to find shade one hot summer afternoon. D.J. pulled out of the driveway, crushing her body under his back tire.

When I raced to the vet, I was surprised that Sunny was still alive, but she couldn't stand. Her internal injuries were tremendous, but the vet thought maybe because she was strong and young, she might make a full recovery. Lacey was at a day camp as I held that dog in my lap and begged God for a miracle to save my daughter's beloved dog. I asked God for wisdom on how to share this news with our brown-eyed girl. Amazingly, Sunny survived the afternoon but had to be transferred to a specialized vet clinic.

When I picked up Lacey that afternoon, I wrapped her in my arms and told her what happened. She sobbed and sobbed. I will never forget Lacey falling to her knees and her cries to God, asking that He might save her beautiful dog. And then the clincher came when she said, "Mama, if she doesn't come home, I will have no reason to get up in the morning. I will be lost without her."

Hours later, our family huddled together and wept when the vet called to tell us Sunny had taken a turn for the worse and passed. Lacey's grief was unbearable. To say she was devastated would be an understatement. For days, my cool, calm, and drama-free kid didn't just cry; she wailed. She ate little. Didn't want to go to school. Lacey became withdrawn. But the part that hurt me the worst was this girl, who always had such a deep faith, started to doubt that God was for her. She felt betrayed by Him and confused as to why He would give her such a special gift and then take it away. *"If God is love Mama, then why did He hurt me like this?"* My heart was wrecked, too. I remember scratching out in my prayer journal, *"God, what you are doing to my daughter feels cruel, and I don't know how to take this pain away from her."*

Through intense prayer, God showed me that what I saw as unfair and callous could be an opportunity to reach my Lacey's heart. And if I was willing, He was inviting me to be a part of it. You see, Sunny's death wasn't really about Sunny's death. It was about my daughter's heart. God was inviting me to minister to my daughter through her pain. Jesus wanted to become her source of comfort and strength. He wanted to become her reason to live.

Nearly every night for the next two months, I sat on the edge of Lacey's bed and spoke the Holy Scriptures over her. We talked about God's protection and His faithfulness. We unpacked the story of sin- how Jesus Christ has redeemed the fallen and how God's mercy is offered to everyone. We studied verses about how Jesus is our ultimate comforter and how He bleeds alongside us when we suffer. I would catch Lacey's eye at random moments in the day when we were unloading dishes or driving in the van and whisper God's love over her.

Some nights, I just held Lacey as she wept and confided to me all of her hurt and disappointment that God had allowed this to happen to her. I would whisper strong words of encouragement over her, reminding my beautiful girl that her dignity comes from being God's beloved daughter and that God was weeping alongside her wounded heart. This was not easy. It wrecked me. Because when our kid has a broken heart, our Mama's heart is shattered too. But the Scriptures brought us continual comfort. They reminded us of God's presence and power. Psalm 91:1-2 says, "Whoever dwells in the shelter of the Most High will rest in the shadow of the Almighty. I will say of the Lord, He is my refuge and my fortress, my God, in whom I trust."

Lacey and I learned together how to bring our grief before the Lord and find blessing in it. We leaned into God's truth that He promises to be near to the brokenhearted. We also purposefully began the habit of counting blessings. Yes, she had lost her beloved puppy, but God supplied so many other gifts. We began to list them together, and gratitude shifted our perspective. Together, we learned that true joy is only found in gratitude.

Psalm 18:19-20 became our mantra, "The Lord became my protector. He brought me out to a place of freedom. He saved me because He delighted in me. The Lord is my STAY." And little by little, Lacey's heart started to heal. God grew a tenderness in her that did not exist before. She now reaches out to those who are ill or in pain with mercy and compassion. Just recently, as Lacey cuddled our newest fur-ball addition, Penny, she prayed, *"Jesus, thank you for what you taught me through those trials of losing Sunny. And thank you so much that Mama and I are so close because of it. Mama trusted you, and now I trust you. I know you are for me, God. And I love you with all of my heart."*

That hidden fear you are most afraid of happening to your child? That panic you keep hidden close to your chest…the one that takes your breath away that you just plead with God all of the time to not let happen because it might devastate your child and maybe even turn him away from God?

Stop running from it and invite Jesus into it.

That learning disability your child has?

That stubborn toddler who refuses to be potty trained?

That (immature) woman your son insists on marrying?

That stack of college applications your daughter is crying over?

That acne your middle schooler is so determined to hide?

That team your son just got cut from?

That very thing you most fear for your child may just be the very thing that God will use to capture your child's heart. Something miraculous happens in our mothering hearts when we shift our prayer from, *"God, please, I beg you, do not let this happen…"* to *"God, I trust that whatever you allow to happen to my child will draw him into deeper dependence and intimacy with You Lord."*

My dear friend, author, and speaker Laura has endured an excoriating mothering season of watching one of her children suffer and pull away from how she raised him. Laura's son has battled addiction and been in and out of rehab, leaving Laura feeling heartbroken and totally out of control. I have learned so much from her steadfastness in her faith amid deep heartache, "Here's the thing. We will all have a season, or two or three (but who's counting), when life falls apart. The only thing more painful than your own falling apart is watching your loved one fall apart. And sure, we can try to jump in and save ourselves. We can pretend that our love is enough and we are sufficient. We can throw out the safety net and cushion our loved one's fall as many times as we'd like. But remember, Jesus fell three times on His way to Calvary, and not once did His mother try to prevent the crucifixion from happening. Instead, she followed Him, she kept her eyes on Him, and she stood with Him. And then, she waited for Him to rise. I have to believe we were left with this model for good reason." [2]

When we, as mothers, surrender our plans to the plans of God, we become free to love our children in a new way. We become witnesses and ambassadors of their life journey, not prison guards aimed at protecting them from our every fear. This requires one thing: we have to be available.

Of all the principles of mothering I speak about around the country, I am most convicted about this one. Proverbs 31: 27 says that a woman to be praised, "watches over the activities of her household." Ladies, that means we need to be physically, mentally, and spiritually present with our children to know what is going on!

Former Secretary of State Henry A. Kissinger said, "There can not be a crisis next week. My schedule is already full!" This makes me laugh out loud because I can so relate! An available Mama recognizes that kids often misbehave, or get sick, or need to spill their heart at the most inopportune times. These things that feel like earthly inconveniences are actually heavenly opportunities to shepherd our children's hearts!

Catholic Pediatrician and parenting expert Dr. Meg Meeker says parents' primary question during office visits is, "How can I make my child feel more loved?" Her advice shocks them. She says the number one thing a mother can work on...is her face! Dr. Meeker asks parents to start paying closer attention to their facial expressions when interacting with their children. [3] Children take things personally, so if we are tense and stressed, they believe they are the cause. But if we smile and have warm expressions, they feel love.

Being accessible as mothers is totally counter-cultural and gets a bad rap in our world today of women "doing it all". But I can not emphasize enough what a crucial decision to be available to your children in your mothering. In fact, I beg you to radically limit your screen time in the presence of your children to be open to listening and interacting with them. This is not easy, but it is worth it.

My own Mama was an incredible example of being fully present and available to us growing up. When my brothers raced dirt bikes, my Mom spent the weekends at the track and learned how to change damaged tires. When my sister wanted to grow a garden, my Mama spent hours by her side helping her dig and water plants. When I got my first pony, my Mom got a horse, too, so she could ride alongside me. (And we laughed the entire time trail riding when her horse took off cantering as she screamed at the top of her lungs, flopping out of her saddle!) My mother understood Mother Teresa's words, "Love begins at home. It is not about how much we do...but how much love we put into that action."

In all those mundane moments where my Mom was most available, it made the biggest difference to our hearts. In those everyday, ordinary spaces of life (making dinner or folding our clothes), we always knew there was nowhere else our Mama would rather be than with us. She delighted in us. We felt it. We saw it in her face. And she made everything so much fun. Our Mama was crazy in love with Jesus Christ. In those ordinary moments (in the cracks of time waiting in the drive-thru line or sitting in the basketball bleachers), my Mama would pull out her worn Scriptures from her tote and study the Word of God. I remember her reciting Psalm 31:14-15, "But I trusted in, relied on, and was confident in You, O Lord; I said, You are my God. My times are in your hands."

She never forced us to join her while she read the Bible; she just invited us to listen while she kindly shared what God was teaching her. She always made God's Word interesting and relevant to our lives. And because we loved my Mama, we fell in love with her Savior.

St. John Bosco used this same method of being available to reach the souls of teenagers. He said, "You can do nothing with children unless you win their confidence and love by bringing them into touch with yourself, by breaking through all of the hindrances that keep them at a distance. We must accommodate ourselves to their tastes. We must make ourselves like them."

Even more encouraging is *who* helped birth the passion of St. John Bosco's work to reach hearts for Jesus: his mother, Margherita Occhiena! When she was just twenty-nine, Margherita found herself a young widow caring for three young boys and her ill mother-in-law. She was described as a woman of great faith because God was always on her mind and lips. She taught her sons the catechism and prepared them for their first communion. Margherita had a special place in her heart for fatherless children because she had seen the pain while raising her kids. A wise teacher, she sought the Lord for His wisdom on how to raise three sons with vastly different temperaments.[4] When her son John was called to the priesthood at an early age, she accompanied him there, later working alongside his ministry to reach the lost hearts of young men. Margherita also mothered the kids received by John Bosco, ensuring they were properly provided with nourishment.[5] Margherita stayed ever available to be used by God to influence both the lives of the children she bore and the ones God placed in her path. [6]

Mamas, those mundane moments throughout the ordinary days that feel so unimportant? They are the sacred moments in disguise when we can most reach our children's hearts.

I love what Sally Clarkson says in *The Mission of Motherhood*, "I've come to appreciate the importance of the many thousands of routine moments in a mother's life, for it is in these moments that real greatness tends to be taught and caught. It is certainly important to grasp the great calling of motherhood and to respond to a vision of what a family can be. But how I respond to my children in everyday moments gives me the best chance of winning their hearts. If I have the integrity and patience in the small moments of life that are so important to my children, and if I approach them with a servant's heart, then I have a far better chance of influencing them in the larger and more critical issues of life." [7]

God invites you as a mother to shepherd your child's heart through their struggles. But God is parenting you, too! I love what missionary Elizabeth Elliot said: "The process of shaping the child, shapes also the mother herself. Reverence for her sacred burden calls her to all that is pure and good, that she may teach primarily by her own humble, daily example." [8]

I've learned the principle that my most sacred mothering opportunities to love my children can not be scripted. I must be available. God uses many of our most frustrating parenting struggles as tender moments for our own hearts. Mothering helps us grow in humility. Humble, confessing mothers encourage their children to be humble and confessing too. It gives us opportunities to talk about the rescuing love of Jesus and why we so desperately need it. Show your children you are available to them. Talk to your children about your struggle with sin. Share about the forgiveness you have experienced from a merciful Jesus. The degree of softness and availability of our own mothering hearts will create an environment where our children have teachable hearts, too. And that, my friend, is irreplaceable.

11

Audience of One

"There is nothing small in the service of God."
St Francis de Sales

When I was about twelve, I sat cross-legged on our worn, wooden floor, watching her intently. My Mama leaned her face closer to the bathroom mirror. She was putting on her black mascara.

It was July. And wickedly hot. The highlight of our day would come later, after lunch, when we would visit the "neighborhood" pool - the one in our own backyard. It was another summer day where we would stay home. And for us four kids, those stay-at-home-farm-days were glorious. There were horses, kittens, and fields of budding corn where we played hide-and-seek. We would climb trees, race our bikes, and shoot baskets. The five of us would be home together, all alone, until late afternoon when my Daddy's truck would putz down our long gravel lane.

As I watched my Mama put on her make-up that summer day, I knew we were not expecting any company. I was baffled when she took the time to neatly curl her blonde hair and dab on some blush. I had recently noted that "fixing her face" was part of my Mama's morning routine, and she seemed to take a little extra time getting ready on the days when we were not leaving the farm. And to me and my tween brain, this made no sense at all. Why in the world should my Mama

91

give a lick about what she looked like if we weren't seeing anybody important (just us kids and Papa)?

I was a middle schooler and just starting to pay attention to things like this. One thing I sure did notice? My Mama was beautiful. Everywhere we went, my Mama turned heads. She had a lightbulb smile. She was naturally slender, but welcoming babies had softened her tiny frame. My Mama was constantly complimented on her lovely appearance and was humble about it. She carried herself with confidence. This woman God entrusted to carry me in her womb and shepherd my soul radiated beauty. But she wasn't beautiful because of the expensive products she dabbed onto her face or her meticulously kept clothes. No, that's not why people were attracted to her. There was something different about her...my Mama stood out. It was her spirit, her countenance, her love of Jesus. My Mama was beautiful because of *who* she was living to serve.

Everything my Mama did, she did for an audience of One. There was only one opinion that mattered in her mind. One who guided her and was her source of comfort and strength. She saw every opportunity in her day and life to share the love of Jesus. She had discovered the treasure of the gospel at the age of 25 and wanted everyone else to know it, too. My Mama had given her entire heart to Jesus and prayed that everyone she encountered would make that decision, too. Galatians 5:13 radiated out of her: "For you were called to freedom, brothers. Only do not use your freedom as an opportunity for the flesh, but through love serve one another."

My Mama regularly invited us in to learn from her life source, the Holy Scriptures. She would gather us around her rocking chair and open up the Psalms. We would listen to her read about the heart of David (the same name as the man I would marry and name our only son after). David was flawed, yes, and he was very broken. He understood the human tendency to seek his self-worth in the eyes of men, in the arms of beautiful women. But David was humble, just like my Mama. David lived with a deep desire to worship God and glorify him with every breath. Did David have it easy? No, and neither did my Mama. Her childhood was dominated by pain and trauma. She longed to feel loved. Some stories from her past would make you tremble. She did not know the secure love of a faithful, protective, or loving earthly father or the gentle love of a mother.

As a teenager, my Mama turned to outside attention and praise to get her identity. And because she was beautiful and magnetic, she got it. A lot of it. But her heart was restless and desperate for more. She longed to feel loved. Really loved. And when she discovered the unconditional love of the Creator God, the one who sent His very own son to die and take my Mama's place, my Mama's life was forever changed. She now only needed the approval of One.

While raising us, like David, my Mama returned daily to this humble desire to please God above all else. Her commitment was steadfast. Purposeful. She acted even when she was weary, tired, or discouraged. My Mom mothered with a desire to please God above all else. And that example has left a lasting impression on many souls, especially mine.

My mother found her identity not in her earthly birthright but in her heavenly one. She started a new life, living as the daughter of the Heavenly King, using the rhythm of daily life to shepherd my heart and to teach me more about growing my relationship with Jesus Christ. Just like the day when I asked her why she was putting on mascara when nobody but us crazy kids were going to see her, "Who cares what you look like, Mama? Why does it even matter if no one notices what you do?"

I reached for her hairbrush and attempted to comb through my knots. She paused. Her eyes sparkled. Her words are etched in my heart forever, "You are right, Jo. It does not matter what people think about me. But God cares, Jo. God sees me. I need to be my best today to serve as a mother. And that means getting up, caring for the one body God has given me, and getting ready to work for Jesus. Jesus wants me to live my life to honor him, and I might as well look my best while doing it!"

And once again, she pointed me back to Scripture. "Work with enthusiasm, as though you were working for the Lord rather than for people." (Ephesians 6:7 NLT)

Author Philip Yancey challenges us to become aware of who we turn to find our significance. "Do we clamor for attention and achievement? Jesus invites us to let go of that competitive struggle, to trust that God's opinion of us is the only one that ultimately counts. How would our lives differ if we truly played to an audience of One? Certainly, our sense of ego and rivalry would fade because we would no longer need to worry about proving ourselves to others. We could concentrate instead on pleasing God by living in a way that would attract people to Jesus." [1]

Who are you mothering for today? Who is your audience? Is it Instagram, that other Mama at the playground, or your husband you want approval from? Pause and think about this for one minute. Sit with your heart's answer.

Something miraculously shifts in our hearts when we can admit who or what we are living for and then pray about laying that to the side so we can mother for an audience of One.

When we do this, our entire countenance shifts. Knowing God sees us, we can change that dirty diaper and look up smiling. We can cook that thousandth meal (and accidentally add too much salt), chuckling because we know God is watching. We can pause to laugh at a silly sentence from a toddler because we are not alone; God is hearing it, too. We can lean in and help that middle schooler with his (dreaded) math homework because God is beside us. We can wrap our arms of comfort around that teenager sobbing over that mean group text because God weeps with her, too.

It is in those hidden moments when God can best use us. "The very obscurity in which most of us raise our children, tend our homes, and practice our faith is part of what guards and nurtures growth in sanctity. If the world was watching or if we thought one day our story would be told, we probably could not be dependably detached from our egos in living out the Gospel. To be a mother is intrinsically a vocation to hiddenness, and this fact is perhaps what makes it most potentially sanctifying," notes Allison Ciraulo. [2]

When we see ourselves as instruments in the hands of the Master, it helps us focus our attention on pleasing Him. He then becomes the only audience that matters.[3]. When we mother for an Audience of One, what can feel so mundane becomes miraculous. What feels so unseen becomes a highlight reel of love. Parenting conversations become opportunities to reach our children's hearts. God is our witness to all that feels lonely and hidden.

God sees it all.

I love the story of Hagar in the Old Testament. Like my own Mama, she was wandering, feeling wounded and unseen. Hagar, a pregnant slave abandoned and lost, has an encounter with the living God that reshapes her identity and changes her purpose for living. Hagar meets God at a well and leaves completely transformed. She goes from enslaved to redeemed, proclaiming, "You are the God who sees me...I have now seen the One who sees me." (Genesis 16:13).

Hagar is the only person in the Bible to give a name to God, calling him "the God Who Sees." She discovers that God sees and hears broken women as she spreads the word of the God she met beside the well. Her experience at the well became so widely known that, in time, the well came to be called Beer Lahai Roi, meaning "spring of the living one who sees me." Acting in faith, Hagar returns to Abram and Sarai's household with a different perspective. [4]

You are seen, my dear sister. In the messiness of mothering, in the loneliness, in the dirty dishes and spilled milkshakes and lost homework and unpacked lunches, in the nursing pads and the fussy, teething babies, and in the teenager who today acts like he hates your guts. You are seen in the joyful places and in the mucky ones.

You. Are. Seen.
God. Sees. You.

Nothing goes unnoticed by the Heavenly King. You are his beautiful daughter, and He is simply enamored with you. Not because you are perfect, but because you are perfectly His.

How amazing our mindset would be if we started each day with the simple prayer of David in Psalm 86:10-12: "For you are great and perform wonderful deeds. You alone are God. Teach me your ways, O Lord, that I may live according to your truth! Grant me purity of heart so that I may honor you. With all my heart, I will praise you, O Lord my God. I will give glory to your name forever."

So Mamas? Even though I'll be home most of the day caring for little ones tomorrow, do you know the first thing I'll tackle when my alarm goes off bright and early? Tomorrow, I will get up at first light and shower (plus, like my one friend always says, "Jodi, after all these babies, we look half-dead if we don't put some kinda of something on..."). I will pray for courage for the day and then take a few minutes to get dressed and comb through that (still) messy hair. And why will I do this? Because I have the holy privilege of mothering these four kids. Oh - and an Audience of One is watching everything I do. I want to serve Him and be His earthly ambassador. And maybe do it with a little mascara on...

12

Understanding Your Value: You Are Worth Far More Than You Think

> *"Are we making the right choice when we choose a more comfortable material life for the mental health and well-being of our children and ourselves? Your baby does not care if she has a bigger room or a Florida vacation; what she wants is you and the safety and security of being in your presence."*
>
> Carrie Gress

Tonight, I arrived at my son's basketball practice, laptop tucked under my arm, hoping to steal a few minutes alone to write. God had other plans for me. As I watched the middle-school boys shuffle through defensive slides and shooting drills, my eyes caught a nearby bleacher- Mom wrestling with a wayward toddler. I slid over to say hi and ask how she was doing. She immediately launched into telling me about her frustrating day. She needed to vent, and I completely understand why. The COVID pandemic had wreaked havoc on her kids' school schedule, and she felt like her oldest had fallen far behind in math. A recent move into a new neighborhood had left a trail of unpacked boxes and chaos at home. As if she wasn't busy enough, my friend described her decision to establish a new online business and the inconveniences that came with it. As our boys dribbled up and down the court, she confided her marriage was struggling, and her husband was irritated over her lack of time and affection for him. She was overwhelmed and worn thin.

I listened as she spilled out all of the things on her plate, and then when the conversation quieted between us, I gently asked, "Is your side hustle something you might consider putting on hold for a little bit until you get the house totally settled and have a little more margin to take care of yourself, your children and your husband?" She laughed nervously and then, as if convincing herself more than me, pointed to her son on the basketball court and said, "But I'm doing *all* this so that my kids can have nicer clothes and newer electronics. I'm working all these extra hours to contribute and spend more money at Target. I'm doing all this to make *them* happy!" Our eyes locked, but I sensed there was a deeper layer to her story. I slid my arm around her shoulder and squeezed her tight. Wet tears splashed down her face. I wanted her to know that I saw her struggle with her priorities like God has seen me struggle with mine.

"Tell me more," I said to her, pulling two chocolate granola bars out of my purse and handing her one (because it's a known fact that all moms need chocolate when they are crying over the strain of motherhood). "Tell me a little about your own childhood."

"I never had any new toys as a kid, always thrift toys," she whispered. "It was embarrassing. Not only that, but I was lonely a lot. My parents were always working and busy. I want my kids to have everything I never had." I nodded my head, grateful for her honesty. She continued, "The truth is I don't feel like I matter if I can't buy things for them." I hugged her again, proud of her authenticity and maturity. My friend was unveiling the key motivations of her heart and exposing her insecurity. This takes courage. She believed her motherhood was not enough. She was spinning her wheels trying to do it all but constantly feeling like she was falling short. My next words made her laugh and then crinkle her nose in confusion, her eyes begging for more clarity at my seemingly odd statement, "Mama, you are worth far more than you think. You're chasing a paycheck when God is inviting you to build a Church."

During my early years as a Mom, I struggled with *wanting* motherhood to be my primary vocation but feeling completely worthless if I wasn't contributing financially to our family. It would take over a decade of consistent counseling and spiritual direction for me to discover how my own hidden insecurities were driving where I found my personal value. I had dug a deep rut of finding my core identity and self-worth in the wrong places. When I was in the hidden years of raising babies, with the endless cycles of breastfeeding, diaper changing, bathing, and laundry, I often didn't feel like I was accomplishing much. I certainly wasn't earning a paycheck for my hard work as a mother. I remember sinking to the kitchen floor one afternoon, a baby growing in my womb and a toddler playing nearby, to call my husband on the phone, just to hear his voice. I lingered long enough for him to gently ask me, "Jo, how is your day? Are you *doing* ok?" Words of frustration, doubt, and sadness that I had bottled up for months came spilling out of my mouth. I confided to him that I felt useless and unseen and had wasted my college education and work in television to be home instead. I felt invisible. I knew the babies needed me to be a present and attentive mother, and I knew my commitment to love them was best for them, but this certainly didn't feel best for me. I told him I felt...well, I felt absolutely terrible about myself. I will never forget my husband's words of encouragement, "Jodi, I pray one day you can see that being the mother of our children and my wife is enough. I do not love you for what you do. I love you for who you are. Your work as a mother is worth more than earning a paycheck. I pray you can believe how valuable you are."

Although I appreciated my husband's words, my heart wasn't yet convinced. I had a habit of finding my security in my accomplishments. We all fall into the trap of finding our worth in a counterfeit identity. Author Lisa Brenninkmeyer says there are three core ways of defining ourselves; "by what we do, by what others think of us, and by what we possess." All of those identities place one person at the center; ourselves. [1]

"Our dignity and sense of worth will always be in danger if we live with ourselves at the center. Why? Because we are counting on externals that are always out of our control. We can become sick and therefore unable to produce anything. Others can criticize us. We can lose all we possess. And if that happens, we think we will cease to be lovely and worthwhile. Until we come to a place where we stop defining ourselves in these ways, we will always struggle with our sense of worth." [2]

Through paying attention to my discontent in the early years of motherhood, I learned I was driven by the drum of performance. Before babies, tackling hard things and making good money while doing it became my life's marching orders. I would set hard career goals and work my tail off to achieve them. I felt good about myself the more I contributed financially and the more I was recognized in my profession. I needed to know I could provide and stand on my own two feet. I despised being dependent on anyone, including my husband. I somehow believed the lie that I was only as good as what I could do and how much I could earn.

It took a long while for me to believe what my husband said was true. I believed the loud rallying cry that the mission of a woman is to do everything a man can do. Even though I had the blessing of being raised by an incredible Mama who believed in her irreplaceable role as a mother, the screaming propaganda of the feminist culture raged louder, rattling my identity. In high school and college, I was constantly asked, "What do you want to *be* Jodi when you grow up? What will you do with your life?" The mottos of "women can do it all" and "you must do more than raise children" had sunk their teeth into brainwashing me to think that full-time motherhood was beneath me. I did not understand nor embrace my feminine heart. I believed that to have true value for myself and others, I had to embrace the modern feminist movement. I did not understand my true identity as a woman. I did not see my own value as a mother and my irreplaceable role inside of my own home. God kept tapping my heart and body until I got the message. He wanted to heal me and bring me to the fullness of my true identity. First and foremost, He wanted to teach me who I really am: I am a beloved daughter of God.

Motherhood was the catalyst that revealed I was marching to a beat of a counterfeit identity. Looking into the beautiful blue eyes of my Lillian, feeling her soft face nuzzled against mine, and listening to her breath on my chest began unraveling my fraudulent way of finding my identity in accomplishment. Loving Lillian and receiving her love toward me was my heart's undoing. She didn't care if I was on television. She had no understanding of the size of my paycheck (and still doesn't even know, to the fullest extent, my list of career accolades today). She cared about *me*. She saw *me*. She loved *me* without condition. She delighted in *me*. No strings attached. God used the unconditional love of a tiny baby to reveal His personal, abundant love for me. Motherhood became the soothing balm healing the wounds of my heart. It was not an easy healing process, but I have been transformed because of it.

My friend, do you know *who* you really are? It took years for me to believe my true identity. In my late twenties, a beautiful new friend, Lisa, took me under her wing and encouraged me as I discovered my passion for women's ministry. Lisa helped me uncover those areas where I was finding my self-worth and acknowledge them for what they were: fraudulent identities. This was a humbling and painful process! It took a lot of hard conversations, tears, and soul work to allow God to re-teach my heart to find my true core identity. But because of Lisa's mentorship, my life was transformed through a rebirth of learning who I truly am: God's beloved daughter. Lisa writes about it here, "If only you could truly grasp the depth of God's love for you. If you could, it would satisfy your every longing. It is He that you were born hungering for, hunting for, searching for. Your life is actually a love story, no matter how disappointed you may have been by people falling short. The One who pursued you is the Lover of your soul. He isn't asking you to prove that you are worth something. You don't have to do something spectacular, relevant, or fantastic to earn His love. It's offered as a gift, and he proved that he meant it when He died for you on the cross. Lean into this fundamental truth about your value and your identity." [3]

Learning to believe and live in my true identity was also radically altered by my husband's faithful way of speaking words of truth over me. He would steady me when I would come to him, doubting my decisions, insecure, and feeling ill-equipped for motherhood. D.J. was my anchor, securing me to the foundation of my identity as the beloved daughter of Jesus Christ. That fundamental truth is your identity, too.

Allison Ciraulo says in *Motherhood as a Path to Sainthood*, "To the extent that Christian husbands recognize and affirm the magnificent and holy work their wives do at home and with their children, the cloister of the home may begin to become more visible to the Church in a proper and fruitful way. It is difficult for a mother to become convinced of the eternal value of her domestic life unless her husband is the first one to remind her of the fact. And to the extent that husbands also participate in aspects of the hidden work of the home, co-laboring and co-creating the domestic church alongside their wives, they help to advance the most important enterprise a human being can undertake: to bring the Kingdom of God more fully to earth through self-giving love for others." [4]

Author Holly Pierlot bravely chronicles a similar struggle with understanding her identity. She describes how much personal value she received from working part-time as a catechetics director at a large parish near her home. She was passionate about the work and found it meaningful, even though it meant she had to leave her young children several days a week with a caretaker. Although her parish work was making a difference, she found it frustrating how little influence her material really had on the day-to-day lives of her students. Meanwhile, one of her own children's behavior was suffering at home. Frustrated, she writes how one lightbulb moment changed everything for her, "I couldn't spend more time with these kids. Parents had to be the primary educators of their children; I could not replace them. Finally, in exasperation, I asked myself, "What can I do that will really make a difference in society?" *And the answer led me right back to my own home.*" [5] Holly recognized God was asking her to take an active role in raising her own children before pouring her best time and resources into people outside of her family. This was a turning point in her motherhood.

Holly's questions, wondering where she mattered the most, led her right back to her own address. Her commitment to prioritizing motherhood meant she would have to become wise in how she handled her family's finances. "The heart of this priority is to recognize clearly that even the most mundane work has a high dignity placed upon it by God, and that all we do with our possessions and money is meant to fulfill the stewardship responsibilities God has called us to do." [6]

Holly's revelation mirrors my own, "What a lofty and exciting vocation we have! What dignity was attached to even the most apparently mundane task! Every action we do for or with our children reflects the divine love God showed at creation. My own ignorance of my vocation had hampered me from seeing its beauty before. But now the truth had set me free. No longer did I feel as if I was doing something of lesser importance." [7]

Mama, you are worth so much more than what you can contribute financially to your family or what job you do outside of raising those beautiful babies. Your income does not determine your dignity. You don't need to earn your right to matter in your home and to your children. You are worth so much more than the paycheck you are capable of bringing in. As my friend Lisa says, "If we live as God's beloved daughters, then we'll recognize that all we have is from God, and really belongs to him." [8]

The statistics further prove the principle that we must understand our value. While Americans tend to overestimate the amount of money we need to run our families, American mothers radically underestimate the financial value of their motherhood. A 2021 survey from Salary. com calculated the average salary for a stay-at-home mom, and the number will flabbergast you! Stay-at-home moms should earn upwards of $184,820 per year when you tally up their 106 hours of work per week, putting moms in the same earning-value league with some business CEOs! The total was determined by polling thousands of mothers on the tasks they devote time to daily, from grocery shopping to housekeeping to being an unofficial psychologist and the family CEO. The most time-consuming weekly jobs, according to Insure. com, included childcare (40 hours), cooking (14 hours), driving (9 hours), and "miscellaneous" tasks totaling an additional 40 hours. [9]

Even more encouraging, data collected by Salary.com shows an upside to your career in motherhood - the projected value you contribute to your family by balancing the numerous demanding roles of running your home and being the primary caregiver of your tribe is growing with each year. [10]

When we feel we lack what we want to purchase for our children or home, it helps to be reminded of how much we, Americans, have compared to the rest of the world. Americans profoundly underestimate how rich we are compared to people from around the globe. As surveyed by *The Washington Post*, the average U.S. resident estimated that the global median individual income is about $20,000 a year. "In fact," world statistics show, "the real answer is about a tenth of that figure: roughly $2,100 per year. Similarly, Americans typically place themselves in the top 37% of the world's income distribution. However, the vast majority of U.S. residents rank comfortably in the top 10%." [11]

I am in no way saying that making money or having a side hustle is bad. Many women in the Bible used their gifts and ingenuity to bless their families with extra income. If you are capable, I encourage you to do the same. Each of us has different economic situations and unique circumstances, and many of us have to be creative to help bring in extra money for our family! It is certainly validating and gratifying to use our talents and gifts and be compensated for them (more on this later in the book), which is a good thing!

A few years ago, my children and I started breeding one litter of goldendoodle puppies a year. This little business has brought us such delight and also some extra cash. I love that we can work together and do it with my children at home, teaching them the art of caring for animals, responsibility, and how to earn money for the things they would like to purchase. Raising puppies is tireless, instilling a good work ethic in my children. For eight weeks out of the year, we pour our best effort into cuddling pups and caring for their every need. This has taught my children the value of earning money and saving to buy items they would like to purchase one day. Just today, we sold our last puppy from this litter, and it made me feel a little pep in my step when I cashed the check, knowing that I had earned some spending money for our family!

When deciding which additional tasks to take on that might earn money for our family, we need to constantly check with ourselves and our husbands to see if our endeavors to earn more are a blessing to our family or getting in the way of prioritizing our motherhood. We need to be mindful of discerning the difference between what we *want* and what we *need*. Does choosing to pour my best energy into motherhood during this season mean I might need to "offer up" some of what I'd like to do, buy, pursue, or material goods I'd like to give my children? A big fat *yes*. Just today, I walked into a HomeGoods store, gathered a few gorgeous items that were calling my name, and then put them back after calculating their cost. My son needs running shoes for school because he has outgrown his other pair. Both girls need braces, and we hope to pay in cash. The shoes are a necessity, and the decor items are a wish. I *wanted* new things to decorate my front door but didn't *need* them. I'm learning to discern the difference.

God wants us to use our gifts and ingenuity to bless our families. But when prioritizing work outside of the vocation of motherhood leaves us exhausted, frazzled, short-tempered, and irritated with our kids, it's a sign we are taking on too much and trying to find our significance in temporary things. Perhaps we are busting our tails to provide more money when our kids need more time. So often, our hearts turn to material items, our accomplishments, or acts of self-comfort instead of what matters most in the eternal. Sometimes, when we are working ourselves to the bone to balance it all, we convince ourselves it's about the kids when I think it's more about us running from our own heart wounds or trying to make up for what was lacking from our childhood! I encourage you to reflect on your childhood and identify what wounds might still need healing. Once we discern this, we have to have the confidence and courage to pour our best resources, time, and energy into who matters most. Ask your kids what they most want from you. Their answers might surprise you. My guess is that they want *you*! My kids would rather have a rested, secure Mama who delights and enjoys them than the newest sweatpants from Nike or an Xbox game. Trust me, I've mothered from both sides of this coin, and only one has paid back dividends. Your presence matters the most, not the size of your purse or what you provide. You, Mama, are worth far more than you think!

And here is where the church building comes in. The Catholic Church calls the Christian home "the domestic church" because this is where our children receive the first proclamation of faith. [12] Did you realize that you are running your church by prioritizing the care of your children and your home? The Catechism tells us by prioritizing loving, teaching, evangelizing, and serving the souls at our own address, we are building up the domestic church. It is "a community of grace and prayer, a school of human virtues and of Christian charity." [13]

As a mother, the four walls of your home are where you raise warriors for Christ. You are shepherding future saints. You are building up the church of God. There is no monetary value to this; your work is measured in eternity! This is not something to do "on the side"; this is full-time ministry. I pray you see your value. If you are a mother, God invites you to be a church builder. If only we believed in the value of our calling.

"We have yet to see the age in which lay married people, and mothers in particular, live fully into the magnificent calling they have received, an age in which the Christian mother assumes her role as a minister of the domestic church with the gravitas that the vocation truly demands, "writes Allison Ciraulo. "She is not biding her time, awaiting more ideal circumstances or a loftier call; here and now, if she so chooses, she is on her way." [14]

As I grew in my understanding and knowledge of my value in building and protecting our family's domestic church, the story of how one mother lived her vocation became my guide. When I become weary from mothering, I circle back to her story. In fact, I happened to stumble upon it when I was researching the middle name we gave our youngest daughter, Annabelle, St. Therese of Lisieux.

One of the most popular Christian saints in modern history, St. Therese, famously nicknamed the "Little Flower", was a young girl when God called her into his service as a Carmelite nun. She is known for her humility and desire for souls to come to Christ. I was amazed and inspired to discover who was credited with shepherding Therese's tender heart. It was her mother, Zelie.

I took to Zelie instantly. Even though she lived in the mid-1800s, she was relatable. Honest and fun-loving, she also loved writing, revealing the deepest parts of her heart in letters penned to family and friends. Zelie had an entrepreneurial spirit and a cunning eye for business. She was incredibly industrious, running a successful lace-making operation from home, but her business did not compete with her commitment to motherhood. It complimented it. Zelie's primary mission was to cultivate the hearts of her children. And she had a lot of them. Zelie would give birth to nine babies and have only five daughters survive. Each of her girls would eventually enter religious life.

Zelie took a very active role in her children's education and spiritual teaching. She believed she was ministering to her own domestic church. Her goal was forming her children's character, which she took very seriously. She required her daughters to memorize morning and evening prayers and guided them in this daily offering: "My God, I give you my heart; please accept it that no creature, but You alone, my good Jesus, may possess it." [15]

Zelie kept careful watch over her children's daily activities. She noticed when one needed more affection, correction, or tender care. Zelie keenly observed her children's behavior and frequently stepped in to shepherd their hearts. Things like the destructive habit of children whispering, which might seem trivial to someone else, mattered to her. She taught manners, kindness, and responsibility. She patiently shepherded each of her daughter's feminine hearts.

Zelie was honest about her struggles in mothering, colliding frequently with her strong-willed daughter Leonie. The patient mother was often "dissatisfied" with her daughter's behavior, writing to her sister-in-law that Leonie was "overcome with stubbornness" and "a will of iron."[16] Instead of pushing off the child, Zelie drew her closer to her own heart and poured her best energy into parenting her wayward child, writing, "It is only a mother who can continually show her the love that she needs, and can follow her closely enough to do her constant good." [17]

When Zelie became frustrated or discouraged with her children's behavior, she threw herself into prayer, asking God for His guidance and His wisdom on how to best reach the hearts of her children. On one account, she had tried everything to convince one of her daughters of God's goodness when she became exhausted from parenting. She writes how God used her in that moment, when she was at the end of her rope, to be an instrument of His love to one of her daughters.

"This afternoon, I had her beside me in order to get her to recite some prayers, but she was soon tired of that and begged me: "Mamma, tell me the life of Our Lord!" I had not planned to relate anything; it tires me - my throat is always sore. At last, I made an effort, and I told her the story of Our Lord's life. When I came to the Passion, she began to shed tears. It pleased me to see how she entered into the spirit of it. [18]

Zelie delighted in her children. Her daughters felt seen and enjoyed by her even when she corrected them: "She also liked to see us cheerful and full of life. She even willingly played with us, at the risk of having her own day's work prolonged to midnight or after." [19] I find such inspiration in Zelie's story of how seriously she took her role of building up the domestic church in her home. She believed her value in motherhood was worth more than any quest for income could provide.

Do you believe your worth as a mother is worth more than a monetary paycheck? Where are you getting your value and core identity? Who are you? You are who your Creator God says you are. That is where your significance is found and where you can find confidence. You are who God says you are. You are God's beloved. He sees you and calls you beautiful. He loves every part of you.

My friend, I encourage you today to discern what God might be asking you to lay aside for now to free you up to spend your best time, energy, and affection building your domestic church. A paycheck will never replace your presence in your home. As mothers, we are wise to heed Sirach 33:20, "While you are still alive and have breath in you, do not let anyone take your place." Remember, your value as a mother is worth far more than you think. You are priceless.

13

Soul Shaper

"I may not have the same level of influence that Queen Esther had to change a nation's entire history. But there is a bloodline right under my roof whose history can be changed by my courage to embrace hope in the darkness. It is a small, quiet laying down of my life for the sake of theirs. Here, in this house, I am Queen of the castle, and I will use the power that role gives me to raise up a small nation of gospel warriors, knowing I am here in this place for just such a time as this."

Colleen Connell

As we walked into the indoor pool party, I was nervous about being introduced as the *new* mom to the group of private school mothers. We had recently moved Lilli, our oldest daughter, to a private elementary school for the first grade. I only knew the name of one other Mom, Renee. She was the one who had invited me and our three young children to the pool gathering. We would be swimming. In the dead of winter. With people we didn't know. Sounded like a rip-roaring time to me (enter sarcasm here).

Because snow was on the ground outside, I was bundled head to toe in my warmest cold weather gear. I haphazardly threw my swimsuit into our overflowing pool bag, planning to change after we arrived. When we walked out of the cold air and into the warm pool area, we were hit with a wave of indoor fog, making it difficult to see who was there, especially with so many kids splashing around. Through the haze, I could barely make out the silhouette of my friend Renee sitting on the pool edge near the deep end, surrounded by a cute group of moms sipping cocktails.

Within minutes of our entrance, my barely two-year-old son Tripp disobediently wrangled free of my grasp and excitedly ran past the women chatting. He dangerously dangled his little toes over the pool's edge at the deep end. I called for him to come back, but he didn't listen (this made such a good mothering impression on the women watching his shenanigans). I raised my voice and commanded him to come away from the edge. Instead, to my horror (and with no arm floats or puddle-jumpers on), Tripp looked right at me and leaped into the eight-foot-deep water.

Without thinking, I went into full-on Mama-bear mode. I threw the towels and pool bag to the ground and ran full speed to the deep end. Still dressed in my winter jacket, scarf, snow hat, and heavy boots (picture Baywatch here…if it was filmed in the Arctic circle and with much saggier breasts), I dove headfirst into the water to save him. My only son was literally lying on the bottom of the pool when I scooped him up.

When we came up to the surface, I was gasping for air. Tripp, however, was completely unfazed, giggling, "Mama, that was fun! We do it again?" I couldn't help but laugh out loud. That's when Renee (cocktail in hand) pointed to me and said, "Oh! There's Jodi in the pool… the new Mom I told you about…" I saw all of the women cock their heads (with dry hair) to look at me, their faces twisted in confusion. I wanted to sink back underwater. And then one of them leaned closer to Renee, raised her eyebrow, and asked, "Why in the world is Jodi treading water in her winter coat and snow hat? She even has Ugg boots on!"

Welcome to motherhood. Shepherding these four beautiful souls has required a tremendous amount of work and even requires me to get drenched when I least expect it! Motherhood asks a lot of us. The needs of these kids are ever-changing, and the housework makes me feel like I have the star role in the movie Groundhog Day. But being a Mama is so much more than performing tasks. We have to be careful to not get caught up in doing all of the "things" for our tribe and all of the ways we are perceived by others that we miss pursuing the chief thing: Motherhood is about shaping a soul.

This is a divine calling. As Ginger Hubbard writes, "It's about molding character, building confidence, nurturing, training, and guiding. There is nothing like the influence that a mother has on her child. A mother's influence has enormous potential to shape the person a child becomes, for good or ill." [1]

My friend, it is a privilege to mother. It is an honor to be entrusted with guiding another human being's soul. And that is our primary mission as mothers. We steer hearts. We help point our littles toward their Savior when the world offers shiny and empty distractions instead of eternal hope.

Mothers are soul shapers. In the Scriptures, the term "soul" refers to human *life* or the entire human *person*. [2] *The* Catechism tells us that the "soul" also refers to the innermost aspect of man, that which is the greatest value in him, that by which he is most especially in God's image. "Soul" signifies the *spiritual principle* in man. [3] The Church teaches that parents do not produce a soul; God does. Our children's souls are immortal. It will not perish when it is separated from the body at death, and it will be reunited with the body at the final Resurrection. [4] The time and energy we pour into molding our children's souls has eternal consequences.

Don't believe me about the significance of your mothering and your impact on your children? Ask the greatest thinkers and founders of our country who most governed their childhood hearts and who they honor for their successes. Abe Lincoln described his mother as the person chiefly responsible for all he was or ever hoped to be.[5] God knew Abraham Lincoln would need a warm and affectionate mother to spur him on in his early years. Although Lincoln's mother passed away when he was only nine years old, her love became the foundation of his confidence to lead. Lincoln said, "I remember my mother's prayers and they have followed me. They have clung to me my entire life."

Power-house leader George Washington credited his character and success to one person - his mother. Our first President of the United

States said, "My mother was the most beautiful person I ever saw. All that I am, I owe to my mother. I attribute all my success in life to the moral, intellectual, and physical education I received from her." [6]

That genius and stubborn character, Thomas Edison? God gave him just the mother he needed to calm and inspire him. "My mother was the making of me," said Edison. "She was so true, so sure of me, and I felt that I had someone to live for, someone I best not disappoint." [7]

"Heck, Jodi, that's inspiring and all, but I ain't raising no president here in this house. We'll be lucky if we make it through second grade!" I hear ya, my friend. I really do. But I'm gonna say it again. God has big plans for the soul He has entrusted into your care. You might not see it yet. But He does. And He is inviting you to play an irreplaceable role in shaping the life of your little one.

The soul(s) God has specifically fashioned you to shepherd is made in the image and likeness of God. In Genesis 1:26, God said, "Let us make man in our image, in our likeness." This is obviously an important fact that God wants us to comprehend about our design. He tells us again in Verse 27, "So God created man in his own image, in the image of God he created him; male and female he created them." James 3:9 tells us that we have been made to be like God. The Catechism tells us that man (and woman) occupy a unique place in creation because "God established him in his friendship." [8] Of all the creatures God created, only humans "share in God's own life." [9]

Being made in the image of God, the human individual possesses the *dignity* of a person who is not just something but someone. [10] Our children have an inherited birthright that we need to respect. According to Monsignor Luigi Gaussian, a high school religion teacher throughout the 1950s and 1960s who grounded his teachings in Christianity's two-thousand-year history, respect means "to look at what is before you and perceive another presence." [11] When we look at our sons and daughters, we should also see Jesus Christ. Christ is in them, and we are called to see them the way He sees them in their true freedom and ultimate potential. Your son? He is made in the image of God. He is God's beloved son. Your daughter? She is made in the likeness of the Father who created her. She is God's beloved daughter.

I love the disciples who walked the earth with Jesus because, in their humanity, I see so much of myself! In the Gospel of Luke, an argument started among the disciples as to which of them would be the greatest. Jesus, knowing their thoughts, took a little child and had him stand beside him. Then he said to them, "Whoever welcomes this little child in my name welcomes me; and whoever welcomes me welcomes the one who sent me. For it is the one who is least among you all who is the greatest." (Luke 9:46-47) Do you believe your child was fashioned in God's image and has immeasurable worth? It is true! **The dignity of the soul you have been assigned to mother exemplifies the dignity of God. We have been gifted the opportunity to shape souls for eternity.**

These sacred invitations to influence our children's hearts often come at the most unplanned hours. We need to watch out for these opportunities and wisely capture them. Last night, we lingered, the car still running in our driveway, as I recounted to my husband and two youngest children the details of a recent trip I had taken to speak to a gathering of women in Charlotte, North Carolina. I described the joy of one woman rushing up to me after my talk, saying her heart had been transformed when she had an overwhelming realization of God's love for her.

"My prayer every time I take the podium," I told my family, "is that women will have a personal encounter with Jesus. Because for me, that changed everything." Tripp, now in middle school, spoke up from the back of the vehicle. "Mama, *you've* had an encounter with Jesus in your lifetime? When?"

Chills cascaded down my arms. As any speaker with the privilege of serving in Christian ministry knows, it can sometimes feel easier to share our stories on the road with large audiences than with the people in our homes. Surely, my only son knew parts of my testimony well! I turned to face him and nodded my head, my smile big.

"Can you tell us about it?" He nudged his eight-year-old sister. "Right now? We want to hear!"

For the next half hour, as we sat in our driveway, I passionately told our younger children about how Jesus had rescued me from my sin and invited me into a sacred, intimate friendship with Him. I described in detail how Jesus had personally revealed His love to me, convincing me that my soul could only be truly satisfied in a relationship with Him. My husband shared parts of his story, too. Our kids were mesmerized by our testimonies.

Then I turned to our son, "Have you ever had an encounter with Jesus?" He surprised me when his blue eyes welled up with emotion: "Just recently, on the altar, when I was serving during Mass. I didn't know if I made it up or if it was all in my head until you shared your stories today. Still, I was overwhelmed with the presence of Jesus when the Eucharist was consecrated. I could feel the power of God. I could feel His love for me."

Tears stung my cheeks as I joyfully leaped out of the car and raced to my boy. Grabbing him tight, we embraced, and I prayed over him, thanking God for what He was doing in my son's life.

When I tucked Tripp into bed that night, I pulled out the Holy Scriptures and turned to the gospel of John. In John 1:29, John the Baptist sees Jesus approaching when he proclaims that Jesus is "the Lamb of God, who takes away the sin of the world." I explained to my son that these are the very words spoken at Catholic Mass during the Liturgy of the Eucharist. In this passage, John reminds his followers that he is an eyewitness to the power of the Holy Spirit descending on Jesus like a dove and that Jesus ranks ahead of him. John's message and mission are crystal clear: to make Jesus known (John 1:31). John ends the passage, reiterating his assignment, "Now I have seen and testified that he is the Son of God" (John 1:34).

As I knelt at my son's bed to pray over him, I reminded him of Psalm 66:16, "Come and hear, all you who fear God, and I will tell what he has done for me." When we personally encounter Jesus, it moves us to testify to our children. **Each moment of our life is an opportunity to have an encounter with Jesus, an invitation to experience His abundant love for us.** Encountering God may occur on a mountaintop (like Moses), but often, God speaks to our hearts and the hearts of our children during ordinary moments while scrubbing dishes or taking a quiet walk outside. It begins with a desire, a hunger to know God more. An encounter with God often comes when we quiet the noise around us and open our hearts, which the *Catechism of the Catholic Church* calls "the place of encounter" because only "the Spirit of God can fathom the human heart and know it fully." [12]

When we experience God's unconditional love, we are moved to share the gift of God's love with others. This can occur in the ordinary moments of parenting. We can share with our children what God is doing in our personal lives when we are on the way to baseball practice, or cooking dinner, or helping with homework. Lisa Brenninkmeyer writes that as God's witnesses, "We evangelize best when we tell people about our own, personal encounter with the person of Jesus Christ." [13] This looks different for each of us because every encounter is personal and unique.

"Every Christian is challenged, here and now, to be actively engaged in evangelization; indeed, anyone who has truly experienced God's saving love does not need much time or lengthy training to go out and proclaim that love. Every Christian is a missionary to the extent that he or she has encountered the love of God in Christ Jesus," said Pope Francis.[14]

Do you want to help shape your children's souls but are unsure how to practically grow in your faith or share the love of God with your children? My friend, starting today, you can pause and invite Jesus to make Himself known to you. You can ask Jesus to reveal His presence and might to your children. It starts with a conversation with God. The *Catechism* tells us, "Whether we realize it or not, prayer is the encounter of God's thirst with ours. God thirsts that we may thirst for him." [15] You can pray, inviting God to reveal His abundant love for you.

That day, years ago, when my son was disobedient and flung himself into the pool, was not just an embarrassing moment. It was an opportunity to reach his heart (after I pulled him from the bottom of the pool). It would have been easier to chalk up his behavior to just being a toddler. It was inconvenient for me to get him dried off and pull all three of my children into the bathroom to coach them through a valuable lesson: listening to Mama matters. Disobedience can have horrible consequences. I explained to them that God had placed me in charge of them and to honor me and my directions is to honor God. I told my son that if he disobeyed Mama again, he would receive immediate correction and lose the privilege of swimming. Some might say my children were too little for that type of lesson and that type of consequence, but I disagree. We often underestimate the power of our words as mothers. If kids are able to disobey, they are able to obey! When we purposefully and lovingly correct the actions or attitudes of our children, follow through with what we say, and stay consistent, our children will learn to listen. If we lean into those opportunities to shepherd our children's hearts as toddlers, we lay a firm foundation for deeper conversations when they are later teens.

Soul-shaping takes time. It requires us as mothers to be aware of when our children's hearts are tender and moldable. It means wisely capturing teachable moments and leading purposeful conversation. It is not a coincidence when children grow into mature, responsible, and loving adults, they are parented with intention.

"Children do not accidentally become righteous leaders or emotionally healthy and productive adults- any more than seeds thrown randomly to the wind grow to be a part of a thriving garden," writes Sally Clarkson. "Simply throwing children into a cultural tornado and hoping for the best gives them little chance of living up to their potential or coming out unharmed. Someone needs to take responsibility for their nurture, protection, nourishment, intellectual development, manners, recreation, personal needs, and spiritual development. Someone needs to commit time and energy to staying close to them as they grow, encouraging and correcting and teaching." [16]

We, as mothers, have the daily opportunity to guide and shape the souls of the people in our home, both in the toddler years and into the teen years. Now, let's take seriously our role as a soul shaper while there is still time.

14

Delight In Me

"Whatever you are doing, that which makes you feel the most alive, that is where God is."

St. Ignatius of Loyola

When we discovered I was pregnant again, incredible peace and hope flooded my heart. God gifted me tremendous peace. I believed with all my soul that this was His will, and He had heard my cry for one more baby.

After the birth of our son, I endured an intense surgery correcting uterine, bladder, and rectal prolapse. Because of this, our specialist recommended I have a scheduled C-Section to decrease further damage to my pelvis. We also sought out a Catholic doctor to deliver our baby, who shared our faith and understood the complexities of our decision to carry another child in these unique circumstances.

This was a very trying pregnancy, but nothing could steal our joy of learning we were expecting another little girl! God had placed the desire on my heart to have one more baby, and I understood what a privilege it was to carry her. Gratitude steered my heart. I was in preterm labor the entire third trimester, enduring contractions around the clock for months. So it was no surprise that my husband kinda half-believed me when I called him on a cold Wednesday morning in January, telling him I was in active labor.

Our little girl was scheduled for a C-section that coming Friday, but I knew the baby wasn't waiting until then! I had lost my mucus plug, and the contractions had intensified deep into my pelvis. I remember praying all that morning and relying on the example and strength of our blessed mother Mary to give me strength. She, too, had labored in extraordinary circumstances. She would be my guide.

We laugh about it now, but I remember hiding in the downstairs bathroom so that the other children couldn't hear me and whispering over the phone to my husband, "Take a few hours to get your work squared away and prep your clients, because I will wait as long as I can, but this baby is on her way. You've got until after school, honey, and then we are heading to the hospital." I had come such a long way from that first delivery and that detailed birth plan. My, how motherhood matured me. My experience taught me to be flexible during labor (and to sleep and eat as much as possible before the baby comes!)

When we arrived at the hospital later that evening, I was in active labor. As we searched for the maternity floor, we passed a little chapel in the Catholic hospital. I tugged at my husband's arm, and we went inside. And there we knelt as my baby was signaling her impending arrival, in front of the Blessed Sacrament, and prayed over this little soul, the one I had desperately asked our Lord to give us. I remember kneeling and breathing deeply as the contractions came closer together. This memory of us in the chapel has become one of my favorite of our marriage. In the glow of the light of the Eucharist, we each prayed out loud, and D.J. put his strong arms around my belly. God had brought us so far in our faith and understanding of His love for us through the birth of each of our children. Parenting had split our hearts wide open, and loving these children had strengthened our love for one another and our dependence on God.

That pause in the chapel to pray before heading upstairs to triage gave me such strength, strength I did not know I would need. Adoring the Eucharist reminded us of God's sacrifice to give us His only Son, so we might have eternal life with Him. In that quiet moment, God reminded my husband and me what a privilege and responsibility it is to bring a child into the world. He filled us up with His love.

I would love to tell you that the C-section went off without a hitch. But by now, you know me too well. So, I will give you the quick cliff notes.

I was wheeled into the operating room and given a spinal to numb the lower part of my body as the doctor prepped for the surgery. But there was one obvious problem. The spinal only successfully numbed one-half of my body. I remember the anesthetist asking me if I could feel him tapping on my legs when (to his horror) I replied, "Heck, yes!" and lifted my entire left leg up off of the table. His eyes grew wide, and I heard him tell the doctor he would have to put a second spinal block in. I was horrified. I was 8 cm dilated, having heavy contractions, and running out of time. Also, the irony that I was in full-on labor but in the operating room to have a C-section to *avoid* vaginal labor showed me God has an incredible sense of humor (that is just me being polite, God. Your sense of humor is obviously quite twisted sometimes. We will certainly have a chat about this if I make it through those pearly gates.)

I must tell you this next part, but I am typing this in a coffee shop, and I have to make a beeline for the van to finish writing this. Because it's just that sacred to me. And retelling it makes me want to ugly-cry. So first, let me find a tissue.

When the nurses hoisted me up to put the spinal in for a second time, my husband was not allowed in the room, and I honestly started to panic a little bit. Like, I totally mentally came up with a quick plan on how to escape the O.R. and make a run for it. The thought of being cut open to deliver a baby through my abdomen was making me sick, and I was completely second-guessing our plan for a C-Section, especially when my body was in natural labor. I looked at our beautiful doctor and said something mature like, *"Thank you very much, but I think I'll pass on this whole hospital delivery thing and just head back home and deliver there…please get me out of here."* And how did she respond? With such tenderness. And here is where you can grab your tissues. Because what she did next ministered to my heart so deeply.

Dr. Sorra instructed me to wrap my arms around her shoulders and lean on her while the needle was placed in my back. Now, she is a little-bitty-tiny thing, and I am a healthy 5'9", so holding me was not an easy task. My contractions radiated down my body, and I could feel the pressure of the baby coming low. I got the shakes. Like, bad. But she just held me close. Tight. Safe. And she started to whisper quietly, to pray over my body and my labor and over this beautiful baby pushing through. She asked our Lord to be with me, to comfort me, to help my body to relax. I remember breathing her prayer in and allowing it to move into my chest and into my entire soul. And then she softly started to sing.

"Gentle Woman. Quiet light. Morning Star. So strong and bright. Gentle Mother. Peaceful Dove. Teach us wisdom. Teach us love…"

It was as if, in that moment, the entire world stood still. God was with us. Jesus was comforting us. His mother was guiding us. It was one of the most serene moments I have been gifted in this life; it seemed to touch eternity. Amid excruciating physical labor pain, I felt the most interior peace I have ever encountered in this world. God gave me a glimpse of heaven as He, again, called me into motherhood.

St. Therese of Lisieux said, "In trial or difficulty I have recourse to Mother Mary, whose glance alone is enough to dissipate every fear." [1] In that trying moment, I needed a mother who would offer me tenderness, presence, and love. I needed a mother who was irreplaceable. In that moment, God offered me His.

We would name our beautiful girl Annabelle Therese. She was our "little flower". Our miracle. Our gratitude. Our blessing was birthed through brokenness. Anna means "grace," and Belle translates "beautiful." God's beautiful grace had been gifted to us through the birth of this fourth and final child who would come from my womb.

The greatest gift of Annabelle in my life is that she brings out the best in me. I feel her delight in me when we are together. She has a sensitive spirit and is a natural encourager, my best cheerleader. She is a fierce protector of my heart, the first to jump in if anyone around utters an unkind word my way. Mothering Annabelle has given me more freedom to be myself. She has taught me that the best way to minister to my children and serve as God's ambassador is to be…myself! You, too, have been paired on purpose with your child for God's purpose.

Lean into how God wired you and feel the freedom to offer what you are able: the best version of yourself. This means we have to take the time to get to *know* ourselves. St. Teresa of Avila said, "Self-knowledge is so important that, even if you were raised right up to the heavens, I should like you never to relax your cultivation of it." [2]

In her book *MotherStyles*, Janet P. Penley asks mothers to reflect on a time or experience when they felt they were really on top of our mothering game. She invites us to recall "a circumstance where you felt in tune with your child when you were giving him or her exactly what was needed, when you thought with a contented sigh, *This is what makes it all worthwhile.*" [3]

Can you describe what was going on during that time? What were you doing? What was your child doing? How were you engaged together?

"Chances are," Penley writes, "in that moment you were operating from the strengths of your unique mothering style. You were giving your child what you are best equipped to give." [4]

Author Max Lucado calls this our "sweet spot." It's when we operate in our God-given zone of giftedness. [5] Perhaps you are well aware of your mothering style or maybe you are scratching your head wondering if you even have any "sweet spots" at all. I assure you, you do. Ask me how I know? Because 1 Corinthians 12:7 says God "designed" you with specific gifts for "the common good ."St. Paul tells us, "There are different gifts, but the same Spirit. There are different ministries, but the same Lord. There are different ways of working, but the same God works all things in all people." [6]

I'd like to encourage you to take inventory of your motherhood. Have this conversation with a friend or family member you trust. Plato quoted Socrates as saying that the unexamined life is not worth living. When you understand who you are, you can best reach your child's heart. Getting to understand ourselves and how we operate best takes a bit of (uncomfortable) work. It requires taking the time to observe our habits. St. Teresa of Avila said that self-knowledge is a virtue that must never be neglected. Quite bluntly, it means being honest about how God wired us. St. Augustine said, "Know thyself, and thy faults, and thus live." **Motherhood acts as a perfect reflector of our strengths and weaknesses because it is like gazing in a mirror.**

Digesting ancient teachings on the four temperaments and more modern personality typing such as Myers-Briggs and the DISC profile has had a tremendous impact on helping me understand how God has naturally fashioned my soul. But my biggest motherhood takeaway I've applied from the numerous books I've read and podcasts I've studied has been understanding what motivates my soul. I am a work in progress, but God wants me to thrive in being who He designed me to be.

Understanding our God-given temperament, writes authors of the bestseller, *The Temperament God Gave You,* Art and Laraine Bennett, helps us understand our natural inclinations and also grow in our spiritual lives. [7] It does *not*, however, give us an excuse for our bad behavior; rather, it helps us to understand others better, improve our relationships, enlarge our capacity for love, and become more effective in pursuing our goals. [8]

This looks different for each of us. Are you laid-back or quick-tempered? Energized by activity or better off in a quiet atmosphere? Do you respond quickly during conversations or need some quiet time to think before you give your opinion? For example, I might be motivated by spontaneously jumping into our creek in our clothes to teach the kids to swim on a hot afternoon. In contrast, you might be energized by curling up with your toddler and his favorite book on your lap. You might thrive when you organize a group of friends and their kids to take a trip to a pumpkin patch, and I might operate best when I host a peaceful dinner at home.

It's important that we strive to know ourselves. The fundamental feature of learning your temperament is this: people of different temperaments respond to identical stimuli differently. According to Bennett, the way each person responds tends to be consistent throughout his life. Temperament is most easily understood in terms of "patterns of reaction ."[9] It's why planning a large children's birthday party could overwhelm me but stimulate you.

As St. Thomas Aquinas said, "Grace does not destroy nature, but perfects it." Motherhood is a beautiful opportunity to grow my natural temperament closer to the heart of Jesus Christ. And as I do that? My children are watching.

"Our temperament is part of our nature," writes Bennett. "A wounded nature, but nonetheless a nature that can be understood and, with God's help developed... the greater our self-understanding, the better our ability to control and direct our unruly moods and motions...The harmonious and integral development of all the various aspects of our being - both natural and supernatural - will help us lead happier and more productive lives and become more effective in our Christian vocation, and will help propel us more serenely toward our ultimate goal: heaven." [10]

Want to be the best mother you can be? Check in with yourself. Take note of when you are operating from a place of your best energy, when you feel the most in tune with how God wired you to be. And then? Be. You. You are serving best where you matter most when you can accept who God designed you to be, the best version of yourself. As Saint Catherine of Siena said, "Be who God meant you to be, and you will set the world on fire!"

PART III:

THE POSTURE
PROTECTING YOUR CALLING

POSTURE [pos-cher] -*noun*

1. an approach in which someone holds their body

2. a particular way of dealing with something

(See also: 'stance,' 'position', **'attitude'**.)

15

You'd Better Believe… You Are Under Attack!

"Besides all these, taking the shield of faith, with which you can quench all the flaming darts of the Evil One."

Ephesians 6:16

My spunky Lacey only asked for one thing for her birthday: a DudePerfect Bow and Arrow. And let me tell you, I was a little hesitant to get our sassy girl one, but it turns out she's a heck of a good shot. And I have the social media post to prove it.

My "baby brother" Bobby (an avid bowhunter and papa to four littles) was visiting for a cook-out when he was captivated by Lacey's shooting accuracy with her new gift. He watched her line up targets in our backyard, knocking each one down with her plastic arrows. Bobby then got the smashing good idea to use a black sharpie to draw a bullseye on a tougher location to hit, smack dab in the middle of his bare chest. We all gathered around to watch the escapade, laughing our heads off and making bets Lacey would make the mark. My money was all on this fiery girl.

Lacey's first shot was high, knocking Bobby's green hunting camouflage hat clean off his head. I almost peed my pants. I was howling so hard. And then came the second attempt. We held our breath as she set her sight in the middle of the bull's eye, in the center of

Bobby's rib cage. Lace pulled the bow back, and we watched the arrow weave through the air and then make contact with....the center of my brother's face, hitting him square between his eyes on the bridge of his nose. Of course, Bobby dramatically fell to the ground (and this time, I actually did pee my pants. Good reminder to do more Kegels. And yes, this is my family, but like I tell my husband, I had no choice in being related to these people, but he did.)

As mothers, we may not daily literally get popped in the face by arrows (although, you never know what a toddler might throw your way when you aren't looking). But on some days, we certainly can feel like we are sitting ducks in the middle of a shooting range. Dodging arrows. It can feel like we are getting hit left and right. It can seem like our commitment to living out the principles of mothering is under attack.

All kidding aside, listen carefully, please. If you are a mother and a follower of Jesus Christ, let's get this straight on the record. If you feel like you are under attack, it's because you are. You have an enemy trying to take you out. For real. If you are giving your best energy to your children in hopes of raising Christian warriors, you are a target. A big one. And the arrows from the enemies are relentless.

The enemy of our soul, as St. Ignatius puts it, ain't no nice guy. He doesn't play fair. His story is one laced with sorrow and striving. But mostly jealousy. Here's a quick theological backstory. God created the angels, and they were good. But the angel Lucifer saw that God created something even more spectacular than angels, and it infuriated him. God made man and woman in His image to share in His divine nature, and Lucifer was wickedly jealous. However, Lucifer is not envious of God. The enemy is envious of *you* because God created you to share in His divinity. And so he, and a legion of fallen angels he convinced to side with him, waged war. Their war is not against God, for they know God is a sovereign and mighty Creator. **The enemy's arrows of war are aimed at you.** You, God's prized Creation. His masterpiece. The apple of His eye. You, whom God has invited to share in His eternal love in the sacredness of the Trinity.

The enemy is out to take you down. To wreck your joy. To make you waver in your calling to raise these little ones God has placed in your care. **The enemy wants to distract you from seeing motherhood as a privilege. He wants to distract you from raising holy and faith-filled children.**

And where does the enemy aim his vicious arrows? He zeros in on your most tender asset, the birthplace of your motherhood. He shoots straight for your heart. He crouches low and waits until you are worn down, too busy, insecure, and overwhelmed, and then, he lets the arrow fly straight to rattle your core identity. He wants you to forget who you are. He wants you to forget who you belong to and why you are mothering. He wants you to forsake your first love, the love of Jesus Christ. He. Is. Out. To. Discourage. You.

He wants you to feel replaceable. He's working overtime to get you to believe the lie that what you have to offer your kiddos is nothing in comparison to other moms, especially those you follow on social media. He wants to rob you of your true identity as a Beloved Daughter of God. He wants to shake you down. Take you off your game. And steal your joy.

This is how Jesus describes our enemy in John 10:10 RSV. He is "the thief (who) comes only to steal and kill and destroy." Why is the enemy after you? Because when you lean into your calling to mother and find freedom in being authentically who God designed you to be, your life brings glory to God. And when your tribe watches you and mirrors your faith (and they surely will), the enemy is petrified that your kiddos will make the decision to march for our Lord the way you have. But if the cunning, evil one can distract you from your love of Jesus and your mission to mother? Then he can find a little crack to whisper in all the lies we, as moms, so often believe.

The arrows of our enemy tell us this: We are ill-equipped. Unfit. Too tired. Not virtuous enough. Bored with our calling. Not smart enough. Losers if we devote our best energy to mothering. He lies that we deserve to "check out"; he lures us to live numb. Our enemy whispers fibs that our marriages are awful and our husband is not on our team. Hissing that we are not good mothers. The enemy tells us

God is not for us. He whispers God is not trustworthy. That it's not worth pursuing total intimacy with Him. The enemy wants us to turn to things other than a relationship with God to find our heart's happiness. The evil one waits until we are weary; he distracts us from being fully present with the people God has invited us to love and convinces us to become totally consumed with things we have zero control over before he pounces with the lies. Have you heard the lies?

But here is where the story takes a major turn. Like, this is the best news I could have ever added to the A-block (the first block of a network newscast) when I was a television anchor. We have a rescuer! Jesus Christ put on flesh and came down to take those arrows that were aimed at us. Lamentations 3:58 tells us," You came to my rescue, Lord, and saved my life."

During His ministry on earth, Jesus certainly told parables and performed miracles. He was gentle, patient, and kind. But there is more. Jesus came with one mission in mind. He came to fight for your soul. His death on the Cross and resurrection ended the war raging for our spiritual eternity.

"At this very moment," says Father John Riccardo, "Jesus wants to remind us that you and I matter so much to Him that He thought it was worth it to become a man and go to the cross to contend with the tyrant who is too strong for us." Jesus came to fight to open the gates of heaven. For you Mama. [1]

If Jesus is our ultimate rescuer and redeemer, if He came to battle and win for us, for our hearts, why does our Savior still allow the enemy to shoot arrows at us? So why, then, do we still feel under attack? **Because the war for eternity is won, but there is still a battle raging over the status of our hearts.** Jesus did the work on the Cross. He hung there for our sins. He took the punishment for each of us, the punishment we deserved. Jesus Christ took it on Himself, giving us a doorway into spending forever with God the Father. But we have to choose to walk through it. We must choose to confess our sins, acknowledge our need for a rescuer, and offer Jesus Christ our hearts.

And that is why the enemy is still shooting at us. He wants to keep us preoccupied from walking in a close relationship with our rescuer.

He wants us distracted from God's merciful invitation to spend all of eternity with Him in heaven. He does not want us to share in the divine love of the Trinity. He wants us to walk in the dark.

How do we practically, daily ward off this spiritual attack aimed to pierce the joy of our mothering? Our power is in our posture. To protect our sacred calling to motherhood, we must wake up every morning in a defensive stance. We must choose to roll our shoulders back, tip our chin high, and alert our eyes to ward off any spiritual assailant. We must decide to keep our priorities straight, offer God our hearts, and seek His will for our coming day at first light. Faithfully getting up to spend time with our Lord in prayer and reading His Holy Scripture is not easy, and I am a work in progress. When my alarm goes off, I often make excuses and hit the snooze button far too often. But the best things are not the easy things. The best things are hard things. Hard things take decisive action. I want to be a woman who doesn't run from the hard things but embraces them. I want my heart to change to become more like the heart of Jesus. I want to answer "yes" to God's invitation to grow closer to Him, to stand firm in my calling to mother.

In high school, I participated in the Miss Maryland Teen Pageant. My Mama hired a coach to help me learn how to walk the stage. I was good at shooting a basketball, not walking in an evening gown, and I had much to learn. I remember the sting of my coach's voice when she loudly corrected me on how I held my shoulders when I walked the runway. "You don't have a chance in heck to place in this pageant if you stand like that," she said. My face flushed warm. "Everything derives from your posture. You might not feel it on the inside, but how you carry yourself will dictate your confidence. Act confident, secure, and strong, and you will become confident, secure, and strong."

Our confidence in our posture does not come from our beauty, the amount of money in our bank account, how our child behaves in the grocery store, or that last pilates class (although that does help). Those things will fade. Our posture is modeled after that of Christ Jesus. Humble, yet strong. Secure in our identity. Believing we are loved. Not for what we do, but who we are. In the Gospel of Matthew 11:29, Jesus tells us, "Learn from me because I am meek and humble of heart." Other Scripture translations use the words "gentle" and "lowly" to describe the heart of Jesus.

Our posture should be one of courage yet meekness. Does using the adjective "meek" to describe our stance sound surprising and perhaps even weak? It did to me, too, until I studied the life of Jesus. Father John Riccardo writes that "meekness" is a word used to describe how to break a horse. It means "strength under control". That is the posture of Jesus. He is gentle yet steadfast. He is passionate yet tender. Jesus stands strong for what matters most, and that is you. "He is the pure power of God, always under control. Everything he does, he does out of love," writes John Riccardo. [2]

When we stand firmly, the enemy has no jurisdiction here, Mama. Say it with me. Out loud. (Don't worry; the kids think you are crazy anyway.) Repeat after me.

The.
Enemy.
Has.
No.
Jurisdiction.
Here.

He and his cunning, ridiculous lies, aimed at stripping the joy from your motherhood, are not welcome. Not in your car. Not in your closet. Not in your kitchen. Not in your marriage bed. Not in your kid's classroom. Not on the soccer field or the dance studio. (And his lies are especially unwelcome in the Target dressing room, the one with the poor lighting).

Lies directed at your core identity and your mission of motherhood are not allowed to penetrate here. And although the Devil is cunning - you, my friend, have something he will never have and can never rob from you. Freedom. You, Mama, have the opportunity to live set free from lies. Because Christ has set you Free. You are rescued. You simply need to reach your hand and heart out to the One who has come to fight for you. The thief comes to destroy, but Jesus came that we might have life and have it "abundantly." (John 10:10).

The enemy is lurking around, wanting to rob you of all the joy you can experience in mothering. He wants to convince you to quit, to delegate your sacred calling to someone else. Because he doesn't want you raising and adding any more warriors fighting for the heavenly kingdom. My husband often says that answering God's invitation to become a mother has made me fierce. God's fierce Warrior. That is the heart of Jesus. I pray you decide to march with me. Because we are marching on the side of victory.

Psalm 91:4 says, "He (God) has covered you with his feathers, under His wings you will find refuge; His faithfulness will be your shield and rampart." It is time to put our defenses up and roll our shoulders back. Let's come and stand in a defensive posture under the protective wings of the eternal victor, Jesus Christ. In this last section, let's identify the arrows that will come flying at us if we courageously live out our calling to mother where we are most irreplaceable.

16

The Attitude

"Have among yourselves the same attitude that is also yours in Christ Jesus."

Philippians 2:5 (USCCB)

The truth is that even when you are mothering from a defensive posture, trying to deflect the enemy's arrows, there will be minutes, hours, and sometimes days when you simply do not feel up to the task of mothering. Days, which sometimes stretch into weeks, where you quite honestly want to do something (anything!) other than mother because you feel so uninspired to raise your own kids. How do I know this? Because I have felt it. Often.

In fact, as I type this, I am having one of those days today. My attitude simply stinks. I am muddling through an afternoon where I would simply rather be *anywhere* else than stuck at home, warming up frozen waffles, refereeing battles over Duplo blocks, and reminding my kids (again) why they can't ride the green hoverboard in the house. Oh, and I have three extra neighborhood kiddos roaming our messy third-floor playroom right now, all of whom just informed me that they are hungry, too. Can I get a witness?

I haven't showered or shaved my legs in days because I simply don't have the energy to put on real clothes (or a bra). I feel totally blah, and I have a million things to do to get our crew ready for back-to-school, and I am motivated to do absolutely none of the things. I am having a crappy day.

And this feels wrong to put into a book where I am supposed to be encouraging *you* in your motherhood, but it wasn't until I sat down to write and realized how negatively I was viewing motherhood today that it dawned on me: **I am under attack.** Today, I feel like this whole mothering thing is far from worth it. I feel like getting in bed and pulling the covers over my head (and, of course, plugging the heating pad in because that is my one happiness for the day. Enter dramatic, sad music, and please tell me you feel sorry for me).

This afternoon, I'm over this whole "mothering mission" mantra. I don't "feel" it in me right now. Forget the blog and the talks I've accepted to give on the "beautiful" calling of motherhood next week. Peace. Out. Mamas. I'm over it. I am wondering if there is some way I can overnight these four little humans (and the neighborhood kids) for a few days to the North Pole? (I googled it, it's not possible…worth a try).

And that is exactly how the enemy of my soul wants me to feel. Negative. Discouraged. Self-focused. Complaining. I am falling right into his fiery trap. And here is the proof in writing.

This is how Saint Ignatius described the way the enemy of our souls loves to derail people who are pursuing God: "It is proper to the evil spirit to bite, sadden, and place obstacles, disquieting with false reasons, so that a person may not go forward." [1]

Do you know what I've learned? Today's (flat-out) negative feelings about mothering my children are legit, and I need to acknowledge them. They are an *indicator* of the condition of my heart. But today's yucky mood is not a *dictator* of my vocation to shepherd souls for Jesus. Let me say that again (and in case you've only had one cup of coffee today, I will use simpler terms now). I will not allow my crappy attitude toward motherhood today to deter me from my mission to mother. I love what the Reverend Billy Graham said, "The Christian life is not a constant high. I have my moments of deep discouragement. I have to go to God in prayer with tears in my eyes and say, 'O God, forgive me,' or 'Help me.' [2]

A bad attitude might mean I am worn down or flat-out tired of the same routine or just need to do something fun with some girlfriends to remind myself I am a woman first before a mother. I may just need a good perspective change. Or it might simply mean that I am human and having a frustrating (hormonal) day. For those of us who gave up working full-time to raise our babies, I think we sometimes forget that when we were at the office, we often had cycles of bad days. Mothers have crummy days, too. Sometimes, for no reason. Just because. And that's ok.

The best lesson I've learned when my emotions make me feel ready to throw in the towel on this whole mothering gig comes from a petite woman who hailed around the world as a Christian Saint and secretly desired to wiggle out of her vocation every single day. And thank God she didn't let her struggle with her horrible attitude undermine her mission. Because the world would be radically different and a much darker place if she had listened to her feelings above the call God had placed on her life.

You would never know it, based on the pictures we have hanging around our house of her beautiful, weathered face and peaceful eyes. But Mother Teresa had some crappy days too. Days where she wanted to run away from her calling, not toward it. Days turned into weeks that turned into years, which became 50 years of internal fighting for her mission.

One of the greatest saints who lived during the 20th century understood what suffering through a bad day meant. Mother Teresa recounted how, during a conversation with her Lord, Jesus told her she was "the most incapable person, weak and sinful, but just because you are that, I want to use you for my glory! Wilt thou refuse?" Mother Teresa describes how she disputed this urgent request "and told Jesus to find somebody else, that she was frightened of the hardship and the ridicule she would have to endure. She promised to be a good nun if only he would let her stay in her comfortable convent. But he kept cajoling her, challenging her with the refrain: 'Wilt thou refuse to do this for me?'"

And how did Mother Teresa tackle her feelings of discontent and apathy toward her calling? She kept getting up and asking our Lord for an attitude shift. Faithfully throwing herself at the feet of the Eucharist each morning in quiet prayer. She laid her lackluster feelings at the feet of Jesus and allowed her heart to be led by her will to follow her Savior. If Mother Teresa had allowed her feelings to rule, thousands of poor and dying would have been neglected. And theologians agree that she would never have become a saint. Mother Teresa did not allow her feelings to sway her obedience to God in ministering to others. She was quoted often saying, "Love cannot remain by itself – it has no meaning. Love has to be put into action, and that action is service."

We may not get to decide our emotions, but we do get to decide our attitude. We get to decide our actions. And we have to ask for help. Each time we humbly invite Jesus to give us His loving attitude to replace our nasty ones, we take a tiny step toward building a new habit, one that will help us shift our countenance. In his bestseller *Atomic Habits*, James Clear says, "All big things come from small beginnings. The seed of every habit is a single decision. But as that decision is repeated, a habit sprouts and grows stronger. Roots entrench themselves, and branches grow. The task of breaking a bad habit is like uprooting a powerful oak within us. And the task of building a good habit is like cultivating a delicate flower one day at a time." [3]

When my eyes opened this morning, I could feel a cloud of dread come over my soul. I simply do not feel like serving today. During the summers, our house is a hotbed for neighborhood guests. And almost always, I love it. But if I'm authentic today? I desperately could use someone (ok, or a whole tribe of people) to serve ME. I'm tired of shepherding everyone else.

And then I heard the Lord's voice ringing in my ears. *"Get. Up. Jodi. These little ones need you, and I will fill you up to serve. Let me serve you, my beloved. Hang with me today. I will use you today to bring me glory if you are willing. Your part? Simply get up. Put one foot in front of the other. And let me do the rest."*

It's late afternoon now, and I'm sitting down (surrounded by plastic kitchen play food scattered on the couch) to write this reminder to myself of what God is teaching me today (man, He is patient with me!). Because this morning, I got up. And my Lord, my Savior, did not disappoint. Instead, He filled in all the gaps. When I was in most need of rescue, Jesus grabbed hold of me and reminded me how much I needed Him. In fact, the grace and patience that has flowed through this home today is so obviously not cascading out of Mama but coming directly from the Holy Spirit. When I am weak. His strength can radiate through.

Mamas, let's not let our mission to serve be deterred by a crappy day or an uncontrollable circumstance. In fact, let's expect to have them! This world has fallen; we are human, and we are mothers. **Remember, our feelings are indicators, not dictators.** Do not abandon your call to motherhood on account of crazy feelings or pendulum-swinging hormones or the fact that you just found a large black hair growing off the side of your chin or that your youngest just peed on the couch.

Hang in there. Stay the course. You are irreplaceable to your family, especially on the days you do not feel like you are. Do not for one hot minute believe the lies the enemy is pelting your way. There is no substitute for you, even on your worst day. Trust me. (And now I'm off to feed the neighborhood kids lunch…with a smile on my face. But first, I think I'll slip into the bathroom to quickly shave my legs and pluck that chin hair. Oh, and throw on a padded bra because I need all the help I can get in deflecting the enemy's arrows.)

17

Tie Them Together & Kick That Enemy Out

> *"Just for today, I will ask for His grace, the moment I am most repelled by a child's behavior, that is my sign to draw the very closest to that child."*
>
> Ann Voskamp

At the moment, my two youngest "chickens" are sitting together on the bottom hardwood step that leads to the second floor of our farmhouse. Their little hands are tied to one another's with a red bandana. Because they both won't stop arguing. Let's be honest people. I have a chapter to write on the joys of being a mom. Desperate times call for desperate measures. I did what I had to do.

These two have been picking at each other all morning. At breakfast, when Belle asked for more orange juice, Tripp offered to help her and then "accidentally" poured it down the front of her favorite pink shirt. He quickly apologized, but instead of responding with an attitude of forgiveness, Belle started screaming and whining at a decibel that would send even a piglet's devoted mother to the looney bin. I thought we had resolved it (he apologized again and got her a clean shirt while I reminded her she was not a barn animal but a human person). But two minutes later, Annabelle was crying again because Tripp was pretending to be a bee and thought it appropriate to teach his sister what a real sting felt like, playfully pinching her arm. Mama bear again stepped in, giving an animated lesson on how it was not his job to be an ACTUAL BEE and how pinching was simply not tolerated here (even when he asked if, in "fun" instances, such as this one, I could make an exception to his game, to which I answered, "How enjoyable would it be right now if I was a giant wasp who stung you?, to which he answered "Good point Mama. I get it now!" and gently kissed his sister's "sting").

By 8:30 this morning, I had already spent a lot of energy on shepherding my children's hearts. Energy that felt wasted. My middle school girls disagreed over whose turn it was to feed the puppies, asking me to referee. I listened to each side and then tried to gently ask them how Jesus might be inviting them to serve each other. They smiled and raced to do the chore of playing with the puppies together (I mean seriously, playing with eleven golden doodle babies, how we torture them here). When the older girls returned from the barn, Lacey was correcting Tripp over something he had done. Lilli then started correcting Lacey over correcting Tripp. I stepped in and started correcting them all.

The day was not off to a good start. I was feeling worn thin. We needed a reset. So I gathered my four children around the apple tree outside (hoping the fresh spring air would lighten our moods) to remind them that we love each other in this house. Love means that we treat each other the way we would treat a friend at school. We love each other the way Jesus loves us - with tenderness, kindness, and forgiveness. One by one, they sought forgiveness from each other (again). We prayed together for a fresh start.

Satisfied with their reconciliation, I sent my crew to play, subconsciously patting my back at my fine mothering moment. My "glory" lasted five minutes. Lilli came storming in to give me a report on the younger two stirring up trouble with each other again. Her account made my blood boil.

"Mama, Trippy is egging Annabelle on and trying to annoy her. And then Belle is screeching and acting like a baby. I tried to talk to them both, reminding them about what you just said under the tree, but they were acting so…so…uh! Frustrating! You need to come out here, Mama, and do something about this."

And my instant Mama gut? Irritation. I was tired and felt like my attempts to teach them how to get along on this particular day were falling on deaf ears. I was over it. I was tempted to check out. But God was asking me to intervene. So I marched outside because I had had it. It was time to separate them. They had lost the privilege to play together. Surely, that would teach them. They needed time away. I thought maybe send them to their rooms to get some space?

But then the Holy Spirit reminded me of something He had taught me years prior when my oldest girls were in elementary school and had difficulty getting along: *"Jodi, do not push them from each other. Pull them closer. Keep shepherding them how to love when they are most annoyed. This is when I can do my greatest work through you if you are willing to participate. But keep it light!"* Micah 7:8 says, "Rejoice not over me, O my enemy; when I fall, I shall rise; when I sit in darkness, the Lord will be a light to me."

When Tripp and Belle saw me prance toward them, they paused, knowing they were in trouble. I smiled wide and held my arms out wide, inviting Tripp and Belle to run to me. Instead of scolding each of them, I scooped them into my arms. And then I tackled them into the grass, tickling them until they couldn't breathe from laughing. I told my young son and daughter how much I loved them both and that God loved them but that there would be a consequence because they had been stirring up trouble with each other. I watched their little faces turn serious again. I called our dog Penny closer and untied the red bandana from around her neck. And as my children looked on in surprise, I tied their wrists together, telling them they would stay tethered together until lunch. "You are related because you are family and you share the same blood, but more importantly, you need to work together because you share the same God. He wants you to know that when you mistreat each other, you are mistreating Him."

For a long, quiet moment, glancing at their faces, I held my breath, thinking maybe I misheard the Holy Spirit, and this was my WORST MAMA IDEA EVER. But the giggles came fast and furious. She wanted to go to the barn, and he wanted to go to the house. They tugged, attempting to go separate ways, and then my son wrapped his little sister in a bear hug. "We have to work together, BelleBelle."

"But Tripp, if you walk too fast, it will hurt my arm," she told him. "Then I will slow down BelleBelle," he patted her back with his free hand. "But please don't whine. It is making me not want to play with you.. Talk in a big girl voice. We need to work together to make it to lunchtime. Please tell me, and I will slow down."

Tied together, they played legos and built a pillow fort. They laughed their heads off when one had to go to the bathroom. By noon, they were nestled closely together, sharing their goldfish. "Do we have to get untied, Mama? I just love this. Can we stay like this all day?" After lunch, I again smiled wide and untied them, kissing them both. **Acts of unkindness and squabbles pull siblings apart, but motherly love takes the action to draw them closer together.**

Do you find yourself tired from all of the fighting at home? Do you cringe when you hear the way your child talks to you? Have you given up on teaching manners to your kids because they simply won't listen? Do you find yourself saying things like, "I guess all siblings hate each other. This is just part of raising kids," but deep down, you believe there must be a better way? Do you wish your kids showed you and each other more kindness and respect? If you answered yes to any of these, you are not alone. But you are being deceived. The enemy of your soul is at work here. He wants you to feel helpless in creating an environment of peace in your home. The enemy wants you to live in a war zone. It's time to kick that nasty liar out of your house.

A child who obeys his mother from a young age learns the importance of obeying God as he grows. A child who respects his mother will respect his siblings. But children do not naturally obey and respect their parents and each other. They have to be taught. And that is our job. Teaching our children how to love each other is not the job of their school teacher, or coach, or neighbor, or grandparent. It is our responsibility as mothers to foster an environment of respect and kindness in our homes. The enemy wants us to feel defeated, discouraged, and hopeless. He wants us to give up on serving as God's ambassadors. He wants us to be lazy in teaching our children how to love.

So, let's get practical here. What behaviors in our homes should be allowed, and what should not? Thankfully, that decision is not up to us but to God. And what does God say is off-limits? This is where we study His Word to know where He stands. These are God's principles, not our own. 1 John 4:16 tells us, "God is love." Remember, we are God's beloved. God commands us in 1 John 4:11 that because He loved us, "we ought to also love another."

Let's start by defining *what love does not do* before we can teach what *love does.*

Love does not...

Show disrespect. *"So get rid of all evil behavior. Be done with all deceit, hypocrisy, jealousy, and all unkind speech." 1 Peter 2:1*

Lie. *"[Love] does not rejoice in unrighteousness, but rejoices with the truth." 1 Corinthians 13:6*

Hold a grudge. *"In your anger do not sin": Do not let the sun go down while you are still angry." Ephesians 4:26*

Speak unkind words. *"Do not let any unwholesome talk come out of your mouths, but only what is helpful for building others up according to their needs, that it may benefit those who listen." Ephesians 4:29*

Act Rude. *"He who blesses his friend with a loud voice early in the morning, it will be reckoned a curse to him." Proverbs 27:14*

Keep score. *"[Love] keeps no record of wrongs..."*
1 Corinthians 13: 5

Remain Selfish. *"Be devoted to one another in brotherly love; give preference to one another in honor." Romans 12:10*

Act Irritable. *"He who is slow to anger is better than the mighty, and he who rules his spirit, better than he who captures a city." Proverbs 16:32*

Applaud Jealousy. *"Love is as strong as death, its jealously unyielding as the grave. It burns like a blazing fire." Song of Solomon 8:6*

Sin in anger. *"Be angry, and do not sin; ponder in your own hearts on your beds, and be silent." Psalm 4:4*

What does love do?

It always shelters. "[Love] always protects." 1 Corinthians 13:7

Forgives because Christ forgives us. *"What I have forgiven, if I have forgiven anything, I did it for your sakes in the presence of Christ."* 1 Corinthians 2:10

Love acts for an audience of One. *"Whatever you do, work at it with all your heart as working for the Lord, not for men."* Ephesians 6:7

Celebrate each other's gifts. *"What then, brothers? When you come together, each one has a hymn, a lesson, a revelation, a tongue, or an interpretation. Let all things be done for building up."* 1 Corinthians 14:26

Shows patience. *"Be completely humble and gentle; be patient, bearing with one another in love."* Ephesians 4:2

Acts in kindness. *"Be kind to one another, tender-hearted, forgiving each other, just as God in Christ also has forgiven you."* Ephesians 4:32

Chooses encouraging speech. *"Therefore encourage one another and build each other up, just as in fact you are doing."* 1 Thessalonians 5:11

Puts others above ourselves. *"Do not merely look out for your own personal interests, but also for the interests of others."* Philippians 2:4

Is the first to seek forgiveness. *"...the godly...seek reconciliation."* Proverbs 14:9

Believes the best in each other. *"[Love] believes all things, hopes all things."* 1 Corinthians 13:7

Acts Unconditional. *"God demonstrates His own love toward us, in the while we were yet sinners Christ died for us."* Romans 5:8

Understands we can only love through the power of Jesus Christ. *"I can do all things through Christ who strengthens me."* Philippians 4:13

Ultimately, love is knowing Jesus Christ. 1 John 4:9 tells us, "God has sent His only begotten Son into the world so that we might live through Him." What your child says, how he treats you and his siblings, and his behavior are a reflection of his heart. Luke 6:45 says, "For out of the overflow of his heart, his mouth speaks." The Bible says the heart is the depths of one's being, where the person decides for or against God. [1]

Often, what alerts us to our child's need for correction is his poor behavior. But author Tedd Tripp says parents often get "sidetracked" with behavior and neglect what's most important. Bad behavior irritates us and gets our attention. But the problem, warns Tripp, is that behavior becomes our focus. What do we lose sight of? Our child's heart. [2]

The enemy wants you to focus on your child's behavior and neglect shepherding his heart. Now, behavior matters. God's law tells us that. But as mothers, we must be willing to look beneath the bad actions of our children to see what lies deep below. This takes time, understanding the sin traps we all fall into, and requires us to ask for wisdom from God.

When siblings aren't making the right choice to get along, we often need a creative way to encourage them to work together instead of a serious scolding. There definitely are times in the midst of a sibling squabble when it is wise for the offended person to have the option to walk away for a few minutes to cool off instead of retaliating in anger. But more often than not, when parents separate disgruntled brothers or irritated sisters in hopes of squashing a conflict, it actually backfires. The sibling "break" actually delays (and sometimes even grows) the sibling clash instead of reconciling it. And let's get real here for a hot second. We as parents often isolate siblings from each other because we frankly are so frustrated with them (and sick of hearing the growling) that we don't know what else to do. Quite honestly, separating fighting siblings is the easiest choice at the moment. And in making that choice, we send a message to our children that resonates loud and clear: you are destined to fight. It's simply something siblings do. You can not work this out, so I will keep you from each other.

But I say that's all hogwash. And this is where I give you my pep-talk. I believe we can purposefully decide to be ambassadors who do not take the easy parenting route. With the Lord's wisdom and ingenuity, we can shepherd sibling harmony with creativity. In those hardest moments of parenting siblings, we can lean into the power source of God's love and find hope in Galatians 6:9-10, "Let us not grow weary in well-doing, for in due season, we shall reap, if we do not lose heart. So then, as we have opportunity, let us do good to all men, and especially to those who are of the household of faith."

The next time your kiddos are arguing over who gets the Xbox remote, who gets the family car on Friday night, which dolly dress belongs to who, or who gets the brunt work of that dreaded chore, do not give the devil a foothold. Get involved. Be willing to stop what you are doing to talk to your children at that moment, with the aim of getting to their heart. Ask the Lord to lace your language and tone in love. Speak with warm, open arms and a big, fat smile on your face. Pause and say a silent prayer, asking the Lord for guidance in a fun (and surprising) way that might get their attention and force their relationship to grow. Give them the "consequence," and then step back and witness them learn to work and play together.

Just this weekend, my husband and I were quite fed up with a houseful of ungrateful kids on a gorgeous spring weekend. It seemed like everything our children tried to do together created these tense verbal exchanges. Complaining seemed to be the theme of the day. My husband grabbed a few empty painting buckets and quietly handed one to each of our four disgruntled children.

"What are these for Daddy?" the youngest asked.

"If you all have enough energy to whine, you have enough energy to pick dandelions. Our yard is covered in them. If you work together, I'll give you one penny for every weed you collect. But if I hear any complaining, you will earn nothing."

For the next hour, the kids all raced around the yard collecting dandelions, singing as they went. We don't give out money for daily chores, so my husband was perfectly content to pay out a total of $10 divided among the kids when they were done after they counted their stash (counting also became a group effort and took them over 20 minutes so again it was a win-win).

Later that night, when we prayed together as a family, our son said, "Dear Lord, thank you so much that Daddy made us do slave work for him today because it was so much fun. And thank you for putting all of those beautiful dandelions in our yard because I now have four extra dollars in my wallet!"

Lilli winked at me, "Mama, do you remember you made Lacey and me do something similar years ago?" I nodded my head. The details were fuzzy, but I recalled that afternoon because I was pregnant with my fourth child, bone tired, and totally not rocking the mothering game that day. In fact, I remember being at my wit's end. Lilli continued, "I was mad because Lace wanted to play with my doll house, and I didn't want to share my Barbie furniture. You tried to teach us, but we kept arguing. Then you tied our feet together with a big ribbon and said we had to stay that way until we treated each other the way Jesus was calling us to love each other. I remember Lacey begging to sleep in my twin bed with me that night. We ended the day having so much fun."

In my experience, these spontaneous teaching moments have been the ones our children remember and treasure the most. Shepherding acts of love bond our four kids together as friends. You, as a mother, are the primary influencer in your home as well. This role can not be abdicated to someone else. We have to take ownership and understand our parenting guidance can not be handed off to someone else. We have an irreplaceable role in teaching siblings how to get along.

My Mama was amazing at modeling this. She taught my sister, brothers, and me how to respect, love, and forgive each other. As adults, now each of us raising our own families, we continue to treat each other and each other's spouses with kindness and gentleness. We are not perfect, but our friendships are based on humility, and we always strive to reconcile our differences, even when it's painful. This has not happened by accident. It is the fruit of my Mom's obedience to serve as God's ambassador in our lives. She taught us that God called us to see each other as He sees us: His beloved sons and daughters. She never allowed us to go to bed angry with each other. We stayed up until we worked wounds out and sought forgiveness. My husband and I are raising our kids the same way. We have purposefully decided that our home will not feel like a war zone but a place of peace. And the enemy trying to rob us of joy and place animosity among my children? He ain't welcome here.

18

Sleeping With The Enemy

"The love of husband and wife is the force that welds society together."
St. John Chrystostom

With the third quarter clock winding down, I made a mental note of what two things our high school varsity basketball girls needed to adjust to change the momentum of their playoff game. The fixes seemed apparent to me. I was just a young assistant coach, fresh out of playing ball in college. Still, it was easy to see our players were exhausted from playing man-to-man defense the entire game, and our point guard needed to bring the ball up the left side of the court because she was being heavily guarded on the right. Surely, our head coach noticed the same things I did and would address them in the huddle, making adjustments to help us win the game.

Only he didn't. We continued to fall further and further behind. After the start of the fourth quarter, I worked up the nerve to get his attention and whisper my ideas to him. He scrunched his nose, shook his head back and forth, and acted like my suggestions were silly. I was dumbfounded. Weren't we in this coaching thing together? I was there to help, and he completely disregarded my opinion. With two minutes left and still an opportunity to make adjustments and win the game, I approached him again. After all, the championship title was on the line. His stern reply and red face said it all; my input was not welcome.

"I know what's best, Jodi. That will never work. Take your seat. I will make the call."

After the game, our head coach kept a brave face on during the newspaper interviews and in front of our girls in the locker room, but I knew he was dying inside. We hugged and parted ways, ending an incredible season on a disappointing loss. As I went to unlock my car, he called out my name.

"I am gonna regret not listening to your ideas, Jodi. I was so caught up in the moment, and I think my pride got in the way. The other coach told me he was shocked we didn't change our defense to a zone. You wanted to help. You saw something I didn't tonight because your perspective from the bench was different than mine. I guess I was so engrossed with being in charge that I didn't realize we were on the same team."

Just like my head coach should have trusted me with my opinion on what adjustments we should have made during that championship high school basketball game, so should we trust and value the parenting ideas and suggestions made by our husbands. If only I had been wise enough to see how cunning the enemy was in attacking my marriage when I was a young Mama. I wish I had had the maturity to stand firm in the posture of honoring my husband, one I want to encourage you to adopt right now. Your husband is on your team. Although it can feel like it on some days, you (literally) are *not* sleeping with the enemy. Your husband is your greatest ally in raising your kids.

I specifically remember one time when we were on vacation with extended family in Florida. D.J. and I were the first on both sides of our family to have children, and because my husband worked very long hours, I was accustomed to making the majority of the parenting decisions (okay, like *all* of them) with our only daughter. But the chaos of traveling with a toddler to a different time zone, the dynamics of family, and the desire to be a good example had me on edge.

Lilli was just learning to walk as we took a family stroll to a nearby park. As she toddled ahead of us, it looked like her gate was a little off. D.J. said in front of my sister and her new husband, "Jo, it looks like Lilli's new shoes might be too tight. I think we should take them off because she might trip." Instead of hearing D.J.'s opinion as a suggestion, I immediately received it as a criticism. Looking back now, I can see it made me feel insecure that he had noticed something I had not. I loudly fired back, "Her shoes fit fine! I just bought them! I'm with her all day, and I should know best." At that moment, Lilli tripped, landing face-first on the concrete. My sister scooped her up, saying, "I think it's her shoes, JoJo. I think D.J. is right. Maybe consider buying a bigger pair?" I remember that moment well because I was horrified. I was embarrassed by how rudely I had responded to my husband, and I was even more irritated that he was right!

Our spouses love our kids just as much as we do and often have a different vantage point. He sees things differently. And thank goodness, because that is a good thing for both us and the kids. When we care more about our own methods and opinions on parenting and disregard our husband's ideas, at the center is the root sin of pride. Because of our fallen human nature, we all struggle with sin. Pride drives the sin of self-reliance.

Pride refers to a disordered attachment to our own excellence. The proud person tends to seek meaning and fulfillment in her own achievements and conquests. [1] According to Catholic priest and Spiritual Director Father John Bartunek, there are many common manifestations of pride. These include an annoyance with those who contradict me, anger if I don't get my way, impatience or brusqueness in my daily contact with others, nursing grudges, being inflexible, thinking I am the only one who knows how to do things right, unwillingness to let others help and the inflation of my own opinions. [2]

Do any of these manifestations of pride describe you? I certainly recognize many of them in myself. (Writing this chapter is giving me hives.) We all fall into the trap of pride, but for some of us, this wrestling with our tendency toward self-reliance is what some spiritual writers call our "spiritual defect." [3] When we do not confess our pride, it wrecks relationships, especially our marriages. If you recognize yourself struggling with any of the manifestations of pride, that means you are human (and let me just tell you, it's okay if you feel totally nauseated right now because the Holy Spirit is poking you a bit, and this is something you really need to look at. Trust me, this is a "good" type of pain, the kind of conviction that can lead to repentance and transformation)! God has given you marriage as a way to grow in love and holiness. And just like God did with me, He will continue to place you in "opportunities" (often spurred on by your husband) to grow away from self-reliance and into total dependence on Him. Because He loves us too much to let us stay as we are.

So, what is the remedy for pride? It is to focus on growing the opposing virtue on a daily basis. St. Augustine said it best, "There never can have been, and never can be, and there never shall be any sin without pride. The way to Christ is first through humility, second through humility, and third through humility."

Humility comes from the Latin word "humulis," which means "low". Just as St. Therese of Lisieux desired to be "little," the supreme example of humility is Jesus Christ himself. Humility is to place others above ourselves. It is to understand our total dependence on God and our great need for Him to save us from our sins. Humility is knowing we have done nothing to deserve God's love, grace, and mercy.

Embracing humility in our marriage is far from easy because the great battle in every human heart since the fall has been our natural, overwhelming tendency to pride. St. Elizabeth of the Trinity knew this, admitting that "pride is not something that is destroyed with one good blow of the sword!" [4] In her series of spiritual reflections on St. Elizabeth's writings, Claire Dwyer observes, "It takes a lifetime of daily deaths to self to sever the strong string pride wraps around our souls to keep us fastened to ourselves and to keep us complacent and "commonplace" in the spiritual level." [5]

St. Elizabeth believed that when we put on humility, it allows us to move aside so that God can begin His great work: our transformation in Christ. Dwyer adds, "Recreated in Him, our likeness to the divine restored, He is free to work in us, to move beyond the limitations of our nature and to enter the world in great and glorious ways through our 'yes.'" [6]

God has placed you in your marriage as an invitation to grow in humility, and you agreed to be a part of that (remember when you said "yes" as you stood in that beautiful dress holding those flowers?). **I want to remind you that your husband is on your team.** Just like my head coach sought out and invited me to shepherd his team of basketball players because he valued my input, you CHOSE your husband. You decided to make babies with him! You saw things in him that you knew would make a good father. Trust your decision to gift your babies half of your man's DNA. I can pretty much guarantee that the gifts God gave your husband are much different than your natural charisms. And that means the two of you balance each other and can make a great team.

Just this morning, the enemy aimed his arrows at my marriage again. My husband and I were disagreeing over a decision to allow our teenage daughter to play on a travel sports team. He gently expressed his opinion, and although I tried to listen intently, my facial expressions must have said it all. My rude demeanor silently sent the message that I clearly knew what was best, and he did not. I quietly fumed in my head as I loaded the breakfast dishes, and the kids scooted out the door so that D.J. could drive them to school. After all, this motherhood gig was my full-time job. I was with the kids most of the time. I best understood their energy levels, and of course, I knew what basketball team would be best for Lilli.

As the house got quiet, I closed my eyes for a second and took a deep breath. The enemy was at work here. I recognized his cunning voice. He spoke directly to my pride, pestering me to value my opinion over my husband's. He lied to me, telling me D.J. was not on my side. I raced outside to see my husband's vehicle pull out of our driveway. I flagged him down and flung open his truck door. "Babe, please forgive me," I said breathlessly (I can only imagine the scene the poor retired neighbor viewed as she saw me race down the road in my ratty sweat pants and crazy hair. I need to bake that woman some cookies to redeem myself.) "I think you are dead right about this decision for Lilli. Sorry I didn't do a better job listening to your opinion. You are wise, and I trust you." He hugged me back and smiled warmly.

And the devil? Man, he hated what happened between my husband and me this morning because his arrows pinged right off us. When there is forgiveness, humility, and tenderness in a marriage, we give

God glory. When we make it a habit to "give way to the preferences of another," as Ephesians 5 tells us, and stop insisting we do things our way, we give God glory. And when we see our husband as our teammate and not the opposition, the enemy shrinks back.

Not only are you an irreplaceable mother, you are an irreplaceable wife. Your hubby gets only one girl whom he races home to each night, and that's you! Are you making him glad he chose you? Or is your attitude one of self-righteousness that makes him feel more like he is married to a nag than his girlfriend?

The best thing you can do for your children's self-esteem and happiness is to date their Daddy. Make him the highest priority in the house. Care about what he says. Listen when he has an opinion. Love on him. Make him feel wanted. Delight in him.

During this season in your marriage, does reading what I am suggesting make you want to gag? It's okay to be honest with the status of your marriage. But don't stop there. Take inventory of your own heart. Why are you angry with him? I encourage you to have that conversation with Jesus before you start listing your husband's faults. Ask the Lord to show you what you must confess and how to love better. Ask God for the maturity to stop keeping a mental tally sheet of all you are doing against what your husband is not. Ask Jesus to help love through you and to restore your marriage. Do. Not. Quit. On. Your. Man. God has brought the two of you together. Ask Him to be the glue that binds you together.

In the same way, the enemy wants you to forget your core identity of being God's beloved daughter; he wants you to forget you are married to God's beloved son. Your husband is made in the image and likeness of the Holy God. The two of you together encompass many of the complexities of the heart of God. Do you treat your husband like he is the son of the Heavenly King? Because he is. He is royalty because his Papa is the Lord of the Universe. When we prioritize approaching our marriage with a posture of love and protection, when we cherish and applaud who God designed him to be instead of complaining about him, that devotion provides a hedge of protection around our marriage that the enemy's arrows can not penetrate.

19

Ignoring What Stirs Our Hearts

"Knowing Jesus is the best gift a person can ever receive; that we have encountered Him is the best thing that has happened in our lives, and making Him known by our word and deeds is our greatest joy."
Pope Francis

Our kids are climbing up and down a red ladder to the platform. Up and down. Up and down. Another Mama friend and I have gathered at the local park for lunch and playtime, and our eyes are constantly darting between that crazy straight-down hot metal slide and the octagonal contraption where one of my kiddos insists on hanging five feet up in the air upside down.

We watch the kids walk over to the swings, and that's when I finally work up the nerve to tell her what I've been dreaming about. I am beaming as I tell her my idea to host a local retreat for young mothers. Because I have been crafting this idea for some time and want to share my joy.

As I fill her in on all the details, I'm passionately circling my arms...my excitement is brimming over. That is until I notice her face; she isn't smiling. Her mouth is laced with a frown. I mentally retrace my words. Perhaps I said something wrong or didn't explain my vision clearly enough?

Silence falls between us. I take a deep breath and soldier through the conversation, confiding that my talk material is almost all written, and I can't wait to secure the venue. I've been praying about how many women to invite. Does she have any ideas on the music selection?

But I see her eyes glaze over. Our conversation falls flat. I shift nervously from one foot to the other as the sun beats down. And then she says it. "That idea sounds exhausting to me. Coordinating and organizing all of that just to encourage women to be better mothers? No thanks! How will you have the margin to do that when you are so busy with the kids already? And how can you possibly be a good mother, Jodi, if you take the time to plan a retreat?"

I wish I could tell you that I didn't care what she thought, and I was unfazed by her strong opinion on how I should use my time. I wish I could tell you that my friend's flippant response to me sharing my heart's deepest dream didn't matter. But that would be a lie. Because I did care. I cared *deeply*. Because this was a Mama who I respected and loved very much. This was a Mama who had witnessed my journey into motherhood and understood my calling to raise this tribe. This was a friend with whom I was stepping out and sharing what was stirring my heart. And I was crushed by her response.

I pulled my sunglasses down to cover my eyes. I felt the tears sting. What had felt so exciting to share now felt… embarrassing. Perhaps I had gotten it all wrong. I silently scolded myself. Maybe this dream was stupid after all.

Unfortunately (and this part makes me cringe writing this), I let a little lie sink in that day. And I started to live by it. Instead of rolling my shoulders back in a posture of confidence, secure in how God was stirring my heart to serve Him, I sheepishly laid aside my plans to minister to mothers because someone I cared about thought my brainstorm was silly. I laid down something God was tapping on my heart about because *my friend* thought it was exhausting.

I wish I could tell you I was wise enough to protect myself against the enemy's arrows that day. But they pierced deeply, leaving me wounded and weary. For the next year, I closed off a part of my heart and buried a calling. I politely said no to local speaking engagements, halted my plans for the retreat, and stopped writing on my blog at JodiDauses.com.

Do you know what happened when I ignored what God had placed on my heart? I lost my spark. My mothering did not become better. It became monotonous. My service to my children became stale because I stopped dreaming. And a part of me disappeared. **Ironically, ignoring my dream did the very thing my friend convinced me that following my dream would do – it depleted me.**

What I wish my friend had recognized instead and I had the maturity to believe is that God was on the cusp of revealing to me, as author Bill Hybels calls it, my "holy discontent." [1] Our Lord was taking the struggles I faced in the hidden years of raising babies to stir a miraculous ministry in my soul. He was allowing my wounds and deep struggle in understanding how I was irreplaceable to my children to unearth my holy discontent -encouraging the hearts of mothers.

Hybels writes, "Still today, what wrecks the heart of someone who loves God is often the *very thing* God wants to use to fire them up to do something that under normal circumstances they would never attempt to do. It all starts with you finding your holy discontent. It begins with you determining what you just can't stand." [2]

Ignoring my holy discontent drained me. Is ignoring yours draining you? Mama, are you hiding from what God is calling you to step out and do? Hybels says it can be tempting to see what is fractured in this world and be discouraged. We can wonder what one person can do to make a difference in this injustice or to help that abandoned group of people. [3]

Do not for one second believe that your one "small" life is too insignificant to make any real mark. God needs you to lean into your calling to minister to His beloved sons and daughters. God wants to use the very thing you may have most wrestled with or brought you comfort to minister to others.

According to Hybels, if we can unite our angst and frustration to a God who is working through and in people's lives to draw us all closer to Him, we can each become an unstoppable force for good in this world. Our perspective shifts from discouragement to supernatural energy to enter into a God-world view instead of a sin-world view. [4]

"God will often call us to make a difference in an area of life where we have suffered. It is a hard thing to revisit something that has caused us pain. But God doesn't just want to heal us from our past hurts. He wants to restore what we've lost. He wants to bring good from what the devil intended to use for evil," advises Lisa Brenninkmeyer.

"Miscarriage, divorce, grief, abuse, illness, financial loss - these things and many more are faced by countless people every day. Who will minister to them? Those who have been there are going to unquestionably be the most effective at binding up those wounds." [5]

Do not let someone else define and decide what stirs your heart. Be you. Be steadfast in what God is calling you to do. When God and your family support your holy discontent, move forward confidently. Find what energizes your soul and do it. And the people who want to criticize you, hold you back, or tell you that that calling is simply too exhausting? Nod your head, politely thank them for their feedback, and then move on.

Carving out time to pursue your unique holy discontent will energize your mothering, not exhaust it. Yes, God has made you a mother, but you are a woman first. You have callings, talents, ambitions, dreams, and ideas. These are all placed on your heart on purpose by God for His purpose. Pursuing what wrecks your heart for the kingdom of God will make you a better mother. And a better wife. Leaning into your holy discontent will showcase the glory of God.

The entire family benefits when we prioritize using our talents and dreams to further the kingdom of God. Invite your children to serve alongside you. Tell them about what God has placed on your heart. When I carve out purposeful time to live out my heart's calling, my children see the example of prioritizing evangelism, even to the people in our church. And they see that they are not at the center of the world.

Hybels says, "Truth be told, the most inspired, motivated and driven people I know are the ones who lived their lives from the energy of their holy discontent. They have a constant awareness that what is wrecking them is wrecking the heart of God. Refusing to *stay* fed up, though, they instead get fueled by their restless longing for the better-day realities God says are coming soon. They listen to the soulish instinct inside them that says life just doesn't have to be the way that most people experience it. Most importantly, they suit up and jump into the game when God says, "If you'll hook up with me, I'll involve you in effecting some needed change around here!" [6]

What might this look like in your own life? Perhaps it means hosting a sewing circle for pregnant teenagers or teaching Sunday School at your local parish. Maybe it means gathering hungry latch-key middle school boys for a home-cooked meal or bringing coffee to an elderly, shut-in neighbor. What breaks your heart? What would you like to see changed? God might be inviting you to share your beautiful flute playing during Mass, write letters to lonely women in nursing homes, or volunteer at your local homeless shelter. The area that stirs our heart is where our giftedness collides with the tender places of our own story. It's identifying what breaks our hearts and then doing something about it. Embracing our holy discontent is pursuing what God created us to do, not for our fame, but to bring Him glory.

One of the beautiful seasons of my motherhood thus far has been these past few months, as I have asked my children to pray for me as I write this book. My daughters have witnessed me light up at dinner when I tell them the chapter I just finished. My son constantly asks if I am writing stories about him and playfully reminds me he was such an easy baby, and I should tell my readers so! The blessings the members of our entire family experience when Mama is given the margin and freedom to live out her holy discontent have been abundant. Does taking time to pour into my ministry for mothers mean that Daddy had to fly solo to soccer game duties this morning so I could steal away and write? You betcha. (I somehow wound up with my laptop and a stash of books at our local taco dive. Let's just say writing makes Mama hungry. And you should really see what I can scratch out when I order a good sweet tea…) But pursuing time to acknowledge our heart's holy discontent far outweighs any of the minor inconveniences (or restaurant bills). Our mothering vocation can ignite the souls of our children when we carve out a margin to pursue our holy discontent.

Yes, mothering, caring, loving, serving, and teaching my kiddos is my primary vocation. Mothering is sacred. I am irreplaceable to my husband and to my children. In order of my life priorities, first is my spiritual walk with God, next is my marriage, and then mothering. But raising my children is not Mama's only purpose in this life. It is not yours either. We have irreplaceable roles to play to share the Gospel with a fallen world. The enemy wants you to forget that you have a specific calling unique to you to use for God's glory. The enemy wants you to compare your giftedness to the women around you. Do. Not. Fall. For. That. Nasty. Trap. Why does the enemy do this? Because he knows if he can get us to doubt the source of our stirring, he can get us to pull back from our calling. The enemy is out to sabotage us from reaching souls for Jesus. He is shooting arrows directed to discourage you. We must stand firm.

Don't believe me that your Creator is inviting you to share part of what wrecks your heart to reach souls for His eternal kingdom? Check out what God says about this in Ephesians 2:10 (RSV), "For we are his workmanship, created in Christ Jesus for good works, which God prepared beforehand, that we should walk in them." If you are unsure where God is asking you to step out and serve, take inventory of your heart.

"There are a myriad of things that aren't right in the world around us, but if you could help one group of people, who would it be?" asks Lisa Brenninkmeyer. "What issue gets your blood boiling? What brings you to tears or fuels an inner passion for something to change?

Don't allow the immensity of the problem to deter you from making a difference. Before you dwell on the obstacles, try to look at the world through the lens of hope. If you could change one specific area of life, which one would it be?" [7]

Dear Mama, God has specific work just for you to do. Let me rephrase that because this "thing" God has for you? After much prayer, when God gives you the right season and green light to pursue it, it will not feel like "work," but instead like taking a deep breath and exhaling joy. Leaning into your holy discontent is like oxygen. Oxygen for your soul. Oxygen for your mothering.

When I lean into my holy discontent, my children get the best version of their mother. When I am engaged and using my giftedness, my tribe gets a radiant Mama. Because when I am serving in my area of holy discontent, I am most fully alive.

My prayer is that my children get to see a mother who is a good steward of her gifts and that she uses them to share the Gospel of Jesus Christ. There are so many beautiful ways to be creative and serve the Lord. Start small. Take one step. Choose to do the next thing God has placed in your path and do it with intention.

Hosting a retreat or writing a book might scare the pickles out of you. And that's okay. I can live with that. But guess what scares me? The thought of teaching a jewelry class or coming up with a creative snack for your parish VBS campers makes me want to run and put my head under my covers. Mamas, this one life we've been offered is just too short and too sacred to live hidden and scared. Let's celebrate our individual callings instead of criticizing each other's giftedness. Let's step out and serve where God is tapping on our hearts to serve. Let's be a shield for each other, protecting against this arrow from the enemy aimed at discouraging us from living out our holy discontent.

The things that stir our hearts are gifted to us from God to be used for His glory and to draw people to His eternal kingdom. But that's not all. Here's the best part: **God designed our gifts and charism to complement our call to motherhood, not to compete with it.** We can live out our heart's passions and also be good mothers. God doesn't make us choose, but He does ask us to trust Him with His timing and to keep His priorities. Ask the Holy Spirit to give you discernment in this season, to decide how your holy discontent can be woven into your mothering. You've got too much work for the kingdom of God to do, my dear friend. And I'm cheering you on…

20

Irreplaceable, Not Inexhaustible

"All mothers are...slightly insane."

J.D. Salinger

Our black, battered SUV really smelled. Like, so bad was the stank in the air in our vehicle that I rolled down windows and pinched my nose shut with my fingers. I was almost to the Church on a busy day where I was scheduled to give two talks to a women's Bible study group when I had to pull over. The smell in our vehicle was just nasty, and I could not drive a moment farther down the road like this.

As I attempted to pray for a calm voice and focused spirit, this awful smell kept distracting me. With my littlest one in tow, I quickly pulled over at a nearby gas station to search the car. I had to find that smelly culprit before I started dry heaving. I unbuckled Annabelle and, using a funny voice, "inviting" her to play a fun game with me called, "Let's find what smells in the car." She took the bait. As we climbed back together into the third row, we discovered many delightful "treasures": a wad of pink "chewed" gum sticking to the seat, a collection of gray rocks and acorns, three colored pencils, a half-filled red Gatorade bottle, a soccer cleat, and two open containers of Chick-fil-A sauce. Convinced all of these things contributed to the aroma, and after I finished gagging (again), we threw everything into the gas station trashcan and headed for Church.

After I gave my talk, I sat at a round table surrounded by women for a small group discussion. Sitting on either side of me were two young Mamas, each juggling a baby boy on her lap. One started to fuss. After offering to hold him, I noticed this cute little thing desperately needed a diaper change. He. Smelled... Really. Bad. (You see, I'm a pro at this whole diaper/baby/change thing now, so I know my stuff. And this one was a wicked one.)

After taking her little one to the changing room, the young Mama came back scratching her head. "That's so weird. The entire time at our small group table, I smelled something really foul, too. But it's not my baby. His diaper is dry." Well, ladies, I just didn't have the heart to tell her that her baby must have horrific gas!

Later that afternoon, I had my son Tripp on my lap reading books when I caught a whiff, again, of a horrible smell. I grabbed his night-night (blanket) and bent over to sniff it really good. Yep, that thing definitely needed a good hot wash! I immediately threw it into the laundry.

While he went for a nap, I worked at my writing desk. While typing away, I suddenly pinched my nose as I caught a horrible odor hovering near the floor. I checked all around, getting down on my hands and knees to smell the hardwood floorboards. We needed to find a crawl space guy quickly! Something was moldy down there! I made a note to mention this to my husband later.

That particular evening was an unusually busy one in my home. I was about to head off to speak at another church but had to get dinner on the table first and help the kids with their homework. I plopped down on the couch with my husband for the changing of the guard. When I inched closer, my husband put his arm around me, scrunched his face, and waved his hand back and forth in front of his nose.

"Wow, Jo. Something must have gotten spilled on this couch. It really smells here." I jumped up frantically waving my arms as the kids all gathered round.

"I know! This morning, the car smelled something awful, and we could never find out what it was, and this baby I held at Church just smelled terrible. That poor kid's got the nastiest gas! And Tripp's blanket had a horrible odor today. Oh, and don't even get me started talking about the floorboards in our office! Something foul is under there, D.J.. It must be the crawl space. Maybe we have mold down under there? And now it's the couch. It's like the WHOLE WORLD SMELLS TODAY!"

And the room got quiet. Like that. …All five of my family members' heads turned toward me.

"So wait, Jo…WHO is the common denominator in all those encounters today with those nasty smells?"

"Me? What? No way! I showered today. I have on full makeup. Babe, I even put on false eyelashes and perfume this morning for crying out loud! Smell me. Come on, people!!!!" I waved my arms in big circles, inviting my crew to come closer. My kiddos gathered around…all giggling.

And then I looked down at my feet. I was wearing my favorite pair of boots. I had slipped them on at sunlight that morning to take our puppy Biscuit for his walk. And on my feet, they had stayed the entire day. Perhaps I had stepped in some dog mess during that walk? Yes! That had to be what was smelling! Normally, this was my daughter's chore, but I had walked Biscuit this particular morning because he had started the bad habit of picking up everything that crossed his path (sticks, wiffle balls, trash) with his mouth and carrying it around. He needed correction, and I was teaching him how to "drop it."

The kids circled closer as I slowly lifted my foot and sniffed the bottom of my left boot. There was nothing there. I slid it off of my foot. I then inhaled the sole of the right boot. Still nothing. (I then gave my husband that "Martha" look!)

"See! I told y'all it wasn't Mama that smells!"

I grunted (drama is my middle name), took off that second boot, and threw it to the side….And that's when all the screaming started. Before the boot could even hit the hardwood floor, my entire family was practically knocked over by a wave of the most toxic smell. To my horror, I looked down and saw a giant, nasty brownish-red stain on the top of my white dress sock.

All of my kids went running in the opposite direction, yelling and screaming, except for one. Our littlest daughter Annabelle crept closer and started laughing and pointing to what was lying beside my fallen boots on the kitchen floor. And when I saw it, I started to dry-heave and laugh at the same time.

A. DEAD. BABY. BIRD.

I had a DEAD BABY BIRD in my boot for the entire day.

Let me clarify - I had a rotting (with both of his eyeballs still intact) dead baby bird in my boot for the entire day. Biscuit must have picked it up during our walk earlier that morning, and when I said "drop it," he leaned his mouth near my shin and dropped it down into my boot. The dead bird landed on top of my foot. And there it stayed. All. Day. Long.

I thought everyone *else* around me smelled. But. It. Was. All. Me.

As mothers, you are irreplaceable, not inexhaustible. A sign that your life may be on the brink of burnout is when everything and everyone around you seems to stink. The smell of irritation. Amen? When we are stretched to the limit, instead of experiencing a fresh aroma throughout our day, the people we love and projects we take on become a source of irritation. Something minor goes wrong, and it sets us off.

We snap at our spouse. Lose our temper at our middle schooler. Avoid lingering after mass. Yell at the dog. Cringe when the toddler calls our name (again). Some of us withdraw and become passive. We may skip attending a workout, or playgroup, or bible study because the women there drive us too crazy. Some of us isolate and become loners. Some of us overeat, overdrink, or overmedicate. Some of us overwork (me!!!) and then get mad at the people around us when they aren't overworking (me again)!

Irritation? It can be our gauge, telling us our mothering batteries are dangerously low. If I handed you a piece of paper with a black-and-white image of a battery shell and asked you to trace a line of how full (or empty) your soul battery is right now, where would that line fall? Is your soul battery 75% full or nearly all drained? Do this right now, on the margin of this book. Physically drawing this out will bring clarity to your mothering right now.

There was a woman Jesus encountered in Scripture operating with a drained battery. You may have heard her story many times before, but I'm praying that the Holy Spirit has something fresh to whisper to your hearts today from Luke 10, starting with verse 38.

Before jumping into this story, let me give you some context. Here we are picking up the ministry of Jesus Christ of Nazareth, God's only son, fully divine and fully human. When Jesus turned 30 years old, He began His three-year teaching ministry. Jesus had hundreds of followers during this time, including the famous twelve disciples, but he chose three of those men to be in his closest inner friendship circle: Peter, James, and John. However, there were three others, siblings in fact, who were dear friends and supporters of his ministry: Mary, Martha, and Lazarus. They lived in a little suburb of Jerusalem called Bethany, which still exists today.

As we read this, we pick up on a point in Jesus' ministry when he was in high demand. The more He taught, the more followers He gained. The more He performed miracles, healed sinners, and preached parables, the more people wanted from him. His days were increasingly packed. So sometimes, Jesus had to purposefully call a time-out and retreat to get some rest. Where could he do this? At the home of Martha and Mary, He knew He would be among friends. Here, He could wind down and refuel when He was in the company of these two women. So He went to visit Mary and Martha for replenishment.

Here's how Luke describes it, "Now as they went on their way, he entered a village; and a woman named Martha received him into her house. And she had a sister called Mary, who sat at the Lord's feet and listened to his teaching. But Martha was distracted with much serving, and she went to Him and said, "Lord, do you not care that my sister has left me to serve alone? Tell her then to help me." But the Lord answered her, "Martha, Martha, you are anxious and troubled about many things; one thing is needed. Mary has chosen the better part (the good portion), which shall not be taken away from her.""

As you read this, does anybody respond the way my heart does? Do you just feel a bit like Martha gets a bad rap here? Can I get an amen? Here, Jesus and his twelve disciples drop in (without calling or giving a heads-up text!!!) for a "break." These men are dirty and tired and probably flat-out hungry. They are looking for some good old-fashioned cooking and company, and they know where to go!

What does Martha see when Jesus and His entourage arrive? You're right; she panics! That the house isn't in order! I mean, it's one thing for me to host ONE guest unexpectedly…but twelve?!? This is asking a bit much! Right, ladies!?

But in contrast…How does Mary respond? We picture Mary not noticing the mess but embracing the guests! She's throwing up her arms and just going with the flow. Mary pulls up a chair and perhaps says something to Jesus like, "I'm so glad you stopped by! How's it been going on the road? How big a pain have the Pharisees been lately? You can tell us; we're friends. What you share in Bethany, stays in Bethany!" [2]

But there is no sitting for Martha. She is a maniac in the hidden kitchen, frantically trying to get a meal together. She's rattling off a to-do list in her head of all that needs to get done….. "appetizers, entrees, desserts, do I even have enough bowls to feed everyone?"…It begins to grate on her that her sister Mary has the nerve to be seated in the next room lounging while she is working. Martha even ventures to the room where Jesus and Mary are talking just to send a few subtle glances toward her sister…you know…the stare that says, "Get your lazy bum in here and help me!" Cues that her sister doesn't seem to be picking up on!

And then it happens. Martha walks back into the kitchen by herself, surveying everything that needs to be done. She picks up a wooden spoon and starts to turn the simmering soup. This pot is definitely not big enough to feed all of those men! The more she spoons, the more she fumes! Martha snaps. She doesn't even bother to put down the wooden spoon when she bursts back into the room, interrupting the conversation between Jesus and Mary. Her voice is thick with emotion. Martha looks past her sister and into the eyes of Jesus. She hisses,

"Lord... don't you care?" as her face glows red. Martha's eyes spill over with the hot, wet tears of anger.

Can you see the irony here? Martha is addressing the Lord of the universe, the one who left heaven's splendor to put on human flesh, the one who is exhausted from teaching and healing and ministering to sinners, and who will soon bleed and die for the redemption of everyone in the world, including Martha. [3]

And she asks... *"Don't... You... Care....?"* I picture her close to Jesus, wooden spoon raised high, saying, "Tell that no-good-sister-of-mine to help me right now! Before I do something with this spoon!!!" Can you relate? I mean, quite frankly, I am proud of Martha that she didn't throw that spoon like I might have!

And how does Jesus respond to us when we are juggling too much and feel like snapping because we are living in such a state of depletion? With a posture of gentle kindness. Because that's how He responded to Martha, remember? He quietly says her name twice, *"Martha... Martha..."* And then He observes, *"You are worried and upset about many things."*

Jesus can tell Martha is overworked, overwhelmed, overlooked, and exhausted. She's got too much on her plate. Do any of these words describe your soul today? They seem to define our culture, don't they?

Jesus puts his arms around Martha's shoulders. Removes the spoon from her hand and lays it down. He whispers, "You have so much churning up inside of you right now. You're making my visit much more complicated than I want it to be. Can I simplify something for you? When I stop by... it's not for the food. If I wanted a five-star dinner, I could arrange it! I mean, I just fed 5,000 people a few weeks ago with a barley loaf and a few fish! I'm not here for you to rush around and wait on me. When I stop by, it's for friendship. I want to see you. I'm here because I want to connect with you."

Jesus tells Martha, "Few things are needed...indeed ONLY ONE." Martha was missing what mattered most. But Mary got it. Mary had chosen the "better part," the part that had eternal value.

In his book *Simplify*, author Bill Hybels writes that he finds it interesting that the story of Mary and Martha is found in Scripture directly after the parable of the Good Samaritan. He writes, "On the heels of teaching His followers to be active and help those in need, Jesus strikes a different note in his response to Martha's activism. Jesus says, *"In all of your activity… don't lose sight of relationship [with me]"*. [4]

Jesus told Martha that her only hope in battling burnout was to pull up a chair, take a breather from all of the busyness, and begin a conversation with the only One who could restore her soul, settle her spirit, and focus her heart again on WHO mattered. [5] The same is true for us today. St. Paul of the Cross said, "Let us throw ourselves into the ocean of His goodness, where every failing will be canceled and anxiety turned into love." [6]

The best remedy for an irritated spirit who has taken on too much? It is to go first to the only true power that can recharge our batteries. It is to carve out time to be alone with our Lord. But this isn't a one-time charge. Our batteries get drained daily by the troubles and demands of this world. We must plug in every day.

We look to Jesus' example for the best time and way to do this. Mark 1:35-36 "And rising very early in the morning, while it was still dark, He [Jesus] departed and went out to a desolate place, and there He prayed." Take note of three things here: Jesus rose early, He decreased his distractions by going to a desolate place, and He spent time ALONE in prayer.

Scripture is chock full of marvelous activity of God swooping into our circumstances when we meet Him in the morning. Do you remember that it was early in the morning that Abraham rose up with Isaac to go to Mt. Moriah and offer his son as a sacrifice to the Lord? It was early in the morning that Moses was commanded to stand before Pharaoh and say, "Let my people go!" It was early in the morning that the young shepherd boy David left for the battlefield to meet and then defeat the Philistine giant Goliath. And it was early in the morning that the women went to the tomb and discovered that Jesus Christ had risen from the dead.

There are some miraculous things that can happen when you and I get on board early with God. Not just squeezing that time in at some point in the day but consulting Him early in our decision-making process. Early in figuring out what our priorities will be. We just need to get on board early with what God is asking us to do first. [7]

Depending on your kids' ages and needs, getting up earlier than you already do might sound impossible right now. Show yourself some grace. **I have learned that "morning" is a principle, not a specific time of day. It signifies a position of priority, a place of preeminence.** [8] The enemy wants you to consult your email, your social media, or your best friend before you prioritize your time alone with God. Don't fall for that trap. Bible teacher Priscilla Shirer says, "Start each day and each decision with an immediate declaration of complete dependence on Him." [9]

In her diary, *Divine Mercy in my Soul*, St. Maria Faustina projects God saying to her, "My daughter...why do you not tell me about everything that concerns you, even the smallest details? Tell Me about everything, and know that this will give Me great joy. I answered, 'But You know about everything, Lord.' And Jesus replied to me, 'Yes I do know; but you should not excuse yourself with the fact that I know, but with childlike simplicity talk to Me about everything, for my ears and heart are inclined towards you, and your words are dear to Me.'" [10]

CEO Bob Beaudine is a highly successful top sports and entertainment search executive. When asked what he attributes to his international success, this man stuns people when he shares his secret of the "Two Chairs." It's a 10-15 minute appointment that he's kept every morning since 1976. Mr. Beaudine has a quiet place in his home where he has set up two chairs facing each other. Every morning, he comes and sits down in one of the chairs. The other he leaves open for God. For the past 40 years, this top CEO has asked the same three questions, and then he sits in solitude to listen.

Does God know my situation?
Is it too hard for Him to handle?
Does He have a good plan for me?

Mr. Beaudine says this appointment time with God has impacted every major decision he has made in his career and personal life. What would your mothering days look like if you took the time each morning to ask God these same three questions?

As you respond to this calling to serve your children where you are most irreplaceable, God wants you to experience joy. And we need margin in our lives to do that. The smartest way the enemy of your soul attacks your motherhood is that he zaps your margin by enticing you to live a life overloaded with commitments.

According to author and physician Dr. Richard A. Swenson, margin is the space between our load and our limits. It is the amount allowed beyond that which is needed. It is something held in reserve for contingencies or unanticipated situations. Margin is the gap between rest and exhaustion, the space between breathing freely and suffocating. Margin is the opposite of overload. [11]

Having margin in our life is the hero to battling burnout. Burnout is not having enough time to finish the lesson you are preparing for your small group. Margin is having the time to read it twice. Burnout is fatigue. Margin is energy. Burnout is rushing. Margin is hushing. Burnout is anxiety. Margin is security. Burnout is the disease that kills women's lives in this culture. Margin is the cure.

Dr. Swenson adds, "The conditions of modern-day living devour margin. If you are homeless, we send you to a shelter. If you are penniless, we offer you food stamps. If you are breathless, we connect you to oxygen. But if you are margin-less? We give you yet one more thing to do!" [12]

Purposefully adding a margin to our days means we will be living radically differently from the culture around us. My husband and I have made this choice and have fought hard to protect it. It has not been easy. But the cost of living margin-less for my family was just too high. The only way to create margin is to learn to make wise decisions amid endless demands. Put quite simply…We have to get really good at saying NO! And what is the best way to say "NO"? It is to remember that every "NO" is a "YES" to something greater. Saying yes all the time will not make us Wonder Woman. It will make us a worn-out woman. [13]

Mamas, I am so thankful for your willingness to shape souls. This is incredible work. A "yes" that has eternal value. So today, I am asking a bold question. What can you lay down from your calendar this year so that you can say your *best yes* to motherhood? What small yeses can you take off your plate so you have more room to serve well in this *big yes* of ministry to your family? Is this something you would be willing to pray about today? Asking God for His wisdom on how to spend your time best to further His kingdom?

In order to grow and mature in our decision-making process of what to prioritize during this season of life, we need to seek God by having a personal conversation with Him. I love what James 1:4-5 says, "Let perseverance finish its work so that you may be *mature* and complete, not lacking anything. If any of you lacks wisdom, you should ask God, who gives generously to all without finding fault, and it will be given to you."

We must be willing to take things off our calendars to pursue what is most important. You see, if we refuse to release before we add, we will get overloaded. In her book, *The Best Yes,* Lysa Terkeurst writes, "Our decisions are not just isolated choices. Our decisions point our lives in the directions we are about to head. Show me a decision and I'll show you a direction." [14] She goes on to say, "We will have a very hard time paying attention to those BEST YES answers if we live lives that are completely spent. Instead, why not completely spend yourself on the assignments that are yours, those moments you shouldn't dare miss, the calling that pulses in your soul, the love you and only you can offer?" [15]

I love the analogy that author Priscilla Shirer uses in her book, *The Resolution for Women.* She asks us to paint a set of transparent glass boxes in our imagination. Each one is exactly the same size, and each is filled to the same level with a bluish, water-like substance. These boxes are symbolic of the activities of our life, the various undertakings into which we invest our time, talent, and energy. Our tendency is to try keeping them just this way - equally filled with identical amounts of ourselves and our effort. We think that THIS is what balance looks like. But in reality, this is a picture of a woman overworked, frustrated, and exhausted. A life out of balance. [16]

The way we achieve balance is to prayerfully consider God's priorities for us in this current season of life and then rearrange the boxes accordingly - pushing some of them into the background and bringing others to the front. Into these primary boxes, we place the best of ourselves and our effort while perhaps totally emptying some of the others - at least temporarily- not because they are any less significant but because we need to allocate the best of our abilities and attention for the time being.

Priscilla Shirer wisely says, "Balance is not when the boxes are equally filled but when we are free to fill only those that are important for now, without feeling guilt over the ones that we've left for another time and place." [17]

A few years ago, when my kids were not yet in middle school, I had an encounter with another women's ministry speaker that left a lasting impression on me- and it was not a good one. We were speaking at a large women's conference in Virginia when we were summoned to the stage for a mic check before the event commenced. We bantered through some small talk. She had three kids and lived in the midwestern part of the country. We shared a love of animals and I told her about my daughter's new horse. I watched as her phone binged with texts and rang over and over again with calls from her teenage kids. I overheard her respond to a teen who needed help finding her soccer uniform and a son who ran out of gas on the freeway and could not get in touch with his Dad. Her daughter called saying she needed help buying new dress shoes, as this popular speaker assured her it would be just fine.

When her phone was finally silent for a few moments, I saw her take a big inhale and wipe her brow. She told me about her packed speaking schedule, and then I asked, "Is it tough to be on the road that much, especially when you have all the kids busy back at home with school activities?" She paused and plastered on a big smile. Surely, this woman could do it all. And then she surprised me when she looked away from my eyes and said, "Actually, I am missing my daughter's

Homecoming Dance tonight, just to be here. I told myself it was fine because God asked me to minister to all these women. After all, I have dreams too. But my assistant is there helping my oldest daughter with her hair for her big night. And my daughter is a mess. This is so much harder than I thought it would be." That day, as I saw the angst on that speaker's face, I vowed to make a better choice.

When my children were toddlers, I tried to make the best decisions to prioritize mothering their physical, emotional, and spiritual development. This often boiled down to one thing: I needed to be present to them and with them in order to guide them. When I received speaking invitations to share the testimony of God's redeeming love in my life, I filtered them through how my time away from the kids would impact them and my energy level. Surprisingly, as my kids navigate their teenage years, I've felt even more certain about which "box" in my life needs to take one of my highest priorities. My teenagers notice when I am there to support them, when I am rested, when I am available, and when I am horribly distracted. It has been amazing to discover how much my tribe needs a a mother now, some ways even more than when they were little.

During the month of August, I secure my speaking calendar for the Fall and Winter months. I recently was ecstatic to be invited to lead a healing retreat at a parish near our home. I had spoken to this incredible group of women before and was honored they were asking me back. Fortunately, when I checked our family calendar, the date was free, and my husband said he would cover the kids so I could be away that day. As I was responding to the event coordinator that I was available to come to speak, I got a text from my oldest daughter that her volleyball match with her big rival was being moved. You got it... to that very same day. Just to give you some context, this is not just any rival. This is the BIG rival, and this is also my Lilli's senior year. She is the team captain, and this match is one of the highlights of her last year of high school. The matches between these two schools are epic and often decide our conference champion. It would be torture for me to miss it. I called my husband and asked what I should do, and he insisted I should still host the retreat and assured me Lilli would understand, but my heart felt torn. I internally agonized over what to do.

After praying about it, I emailed the event planner and told her I could still come, but I needed to move the evening portion of the retreat a little later so I could be available to attend the first part of Lilli's big volleyball game. I mentally calculated how that day would go (get up super early to drive to the retreat, lead a morning retreat, rush back home to get the kids after school, and then head to Lilli's away match, make sure everyone had dinner on the go, race back to the Church to lead a nightly reflection). Just thinking about it made my chest feel tight. As I waited for a reply from the event coordinator, my anxiety began to tick up slowly. I ignored it for a few days until, finally, I found myself on my knees in our bedroom, asking God for help. It might sound trivial or silly, but I have become very sensitive to listening to my body and noticing the signals when I feel out of control. I have learned the discipline of taking my struggles to God in prayer. That day, I told God that I was fearful I had (again) taken on too much, and I confessed my tendency to over-extend myself. In His tender, loving, beautiful way, God met me there on our gray bedroom carpet and whispered words of love and understanding. As I asked Him for His wisdom, He gently urged me to choose the "better part," I knew He was asking me to have courage and faith to be present where I was most irreplaceable. God wanted me to have the margin to enjoy Lilli's game, but that meant I would have to miss out on leading the evening retreat.

And here is where the story gets really good, and why I believe I have been called to testify about the faithfulness of our Lord. Because first of all, His timing is always divine and He absolutely has an incredible sense of humor. Do you know what happened minutes before I typed the email, bowing out of speaking at the evening portion of that retreat? The Holy Spirit whispered that I should check the volleyball schedule one more time, and wouldn't you know, the athletic director had *just* posted one significant calendar change, that the big game had to be rescheduled the week following my retreat. Hallelujah, good God almighty! I have been learning to adopt a posture of trust, and God is proving He is faithful.

While my kids are still living under my roof, I pray I will stay laser-focused on which "box" I will place my best energy. This often means saying no to really incredible speaking opportunities to be present at their events or home to cook family dinner. But guess what? I am okay with that. In the moment, I feel the sting of missing out, but there is such an abundant peace in serving first where I am most irreplaceable. I have learned when I prioritize who matters most, my anxiety wanes. I have learned the importance of consulting God when my body is feeling the impact of stress or taking on too much and asking Him what I can lay down from my schedule to have more peace. During this season in my life, women's conferences can find another talented speaker, but no one can replace me as my kid's Mama.

Ecclesiastes 3:1 says, "There is a time for everything, and a season for every activity under the heavens." During this time in your life, what boxes can you lay to the side so that you can pour your best energy into the box labeled motherhood? Once we identify those boxes God might be asking us to shelve for now, let's learn to use the two most powerful words, YES and NO, with resounding assurance, graceful clarity, and guided power to serve first and best where we matter most. We do this all so that people may see Jesus when they see us. Hear Jesus when they hear us. And know Jesus when they know us. [18]

21

Forget Your Primary Mission Field? Check Your Driver's License

> *"He intended it to be a fully committed job, not something we do on the side."*
>
> Sally Clarkson

During this season in your life, where are you the most irreplaceable? How is God inviting you to reserve your first and best energy to the people and places where you have the biggest impact?

A few years ago, when my kids were much younger, I was at our children's back-to-school picnic when the Headmaster of our school approached me. "Jodi, we have a big ask for you," she said. "You are the only name that multiple people on our School Board have nominated for this." I smiled because I knew what was coming.

"We need you to chair our annual Spring Auction this year. You'd be so good at organizing and could raise a lot of money for our school." I thanked her for the compliment and then politely said no, quite simply answering, "Saying yes to this is not what is best for my young family for now." She was very sweet. She hugged me and walked away, respecting my "no." I took a deep breath. That was easier than

I thought it would be. I silently thanked God for the small victory of saying no when I am always so tempted to say yes.

Not five minutes later, I was approached again. This time by our school's athletic director. "Jodi, did you get my email? I'm sure you won't mind since you are always surrounded by so many kids and you love sports! We need you to coach our middle school girls' volleyball team. Practice starts this week..."

I took another deep breath. I thanked her for the compliment and then politely said no, kindly telling her, "Saying "yes" to this sounds so fun, but right now, it is not best for my young family." But unlike our school Headmaster, this woman pushed me again, pulling at my heart's strings.

"Oh, come on... what's giving up your time for four hours a week anyway? And I hate to put this pressure on you, but if you don't coach, we will not even be able to have a team at all this year. And you don't want that to happen, do you?" I remember thinking, perhaps this woman should leave her job at school and get into sales! I gently put my hand on her shoulder. This woman was a mother of a slew of older children. Surely, she would understand.

"Thank you again, but I have to pass. My husband and I have decided not to take on anything new this year. It's so hard to say no because you know I love to coach, but I have to be obedient to what God is asking of me. Right now, I need to save the bulk of my energy to care for my four children, and I am already committed to coaching a basketball team! Maybe, during another season, I can coach volleyball. But it's a no, for now, so I can say yes to pouring into my kids and husband."

Her response made the hairs on the back of my neck stand up tall.

"Oh, come on, Jodi. Really? What's your reason? Can't you come up with a better excuse? It's not like any of us really have our priorities in order anyway..."

That afternoon, I heard the Holy Spirit whisper loud and clear again, *"Jodi, what is your primary mission field? Check your driver's license. It's your address. When you say no to outside work, or volunteering, or coaching or extra responsibilities, you are saying YES to the people under your own roof. Continue to get your house in order before you serve outside. Your hurting marriage, your hurting kid, your hurting family...this is always a YES. A yes without guilt and without apology."*

I was telling a friend this story, and she said, "Wow, you must have such good self-esteem and self-discipline to say 'no' so well! I wish I had your confidence!" But saying a solid 'no' to things that will zap my energy and take me away from serving first where I matter most is not a matter of having a boatload of confidence. It's a matter of standing in a posture of strong convictions. Confidence is being more secure in my own abilities. Conviction is being more certain of God's instructions. And because I have spent time in prayer, I know where God is commanding me to put my best effort during this season of my life. **We simply can not do it all.**

Author Allison Ciraulo says, "It should take no convincing for the Catholic mother of small children to believe that she is called to sanctity in the here and now of her labor for her children and household, to believe that the daily tasks she performs in her home can be as much for the glory of God as those of a priest or missionary, and yet I've found it *does* take convincing." [2]

Our spiritual enemy wants you to place mothering low on the priority list. He loves to whisper the lie into our hearts that if we do not say yes to all of these outside asks, no one else will. We are the only ones fit, or else we will let others down. We are irreplaceable. But the truth is that the only location we are truly irreplaceable is our homes and families. No one else can be our husband's wife. No one else can be our children's mother. Let's be women who decide to serve first where we are most irreplaceable. Women who live radically different from the culture around us.

We must remember our true identity does not come from what we do but from who we are. We need to return daily to the truth of who God says we are. The Holy Scriptures tell us of our true identity.

"I am chosen and loved." 1 Thessalonians 1:4
"I am a child of God." John 1:12
"I am not ruled by fear." 2 Timothy 1:7

"I am a friend of Jesus." John 15:15
"I am secure in Him." 1 Peter 1:3-5
"I am loved by God." 1 John 4:10
"I am FREE in Christ." Galatians 5:1

I love what Paul David Tripp writes, "As a Christian parent, no matter what is happening with your kids, you can wake up in the morning and know that YOU are deeply and faithfully loved by the most important person in the universe....Because God loves you, he hasn't left you to your wisdom, strength, and resources...Because he loves you, he works daily to grow and change you so that you are better able to do what he's called you to do....He is present with you in all of his power, grace, and glory so that you can have peace of heart, purpose, and direction, and courage to face your parenting day." [3]

Our posture as a mother is directly connected to where we get our core identity, who we believe God to be, what we think is really important, where we look to find help, and what we look to to give us peace, rest, and security. The way we answer, "Who am I?" will determine how we speak and act toward our children. [4] If we are not resting as mothers in our identity in Jesus, we will look for our identity in our children, in our outside activities, in our accomplishments, or in what we own.

The only way I have practically learned to keep my true core identity front and center is to model the famous sentiment of genius, Sir Issac Newton. I must "keep it before me." St. Paul suggests we do this by guarding the messages our hearts receive from the culture. Romans 12:1-2 says we must "not conform to who or what the world says we are, but be transformed by the renewal of our minds." I need to be reminded daily of the significance of my mothering vocation and my commitment to it. The only way I can do this is to actively abide in Jesus. When I do so, He reminds me of my most sacred priorities. In John 15, 4 Jesus says," Abide in me, and I will abide in you. Just as the branch cannot produce fruit by itself unless it abides in the vine, neither can you unless you abide in me." When I stay close to Jesus, He whispers words of encouragement, reminding me of my primary mission field.

St. Elizabeth of the Trinity said, "The Word of God is the one who gives this command, who expresses this will. Abide in me, not for a few moments, a few hours that pass by, but abide in me in a permanent and habitual way. Abide in me: pray in me, adore in me, love in me, suffer in me, work and act in me. Abide in me in your dealings with anyone and anything, always entering ever more deeply in me."

The choice is up to you. Let's petition God for His priorities for our lives, heeding the words of missionary Elizabeth Elliott, "If we really have too much to do, there are some items on the agenda which God did not put there. Let us submit the list to him to indicate which items we must delete. There is always a time to do the will of God. If we are too busy to do that, we are too busy."

22

Parenting During Unprecedented Times

> *"When we ask, 'Lord, how do I do this? This is hard!' We fall into the lie from the enemy that if we were following the Lord and doing it properly, it shouldn't be hard. But that is a lie!"*
>
> Father Erik Arnold

For many of us, mothering our tribe during the COVID pandemic was beyond challenging. State-mandated shutdowns and long months of school closings stretched most of us thin. The uncertainty of what might be coming next wreaked havoc on our family rhythms. As a mother, I felt pulled in so many directions and was keenly aware of the many needs of my four children during these busy middle years between diapers and college.

Stories of sickness, political unrest, and fear currently sweep our nation. New viruses, school shootings, and racial divisions seem to dominate our newsfeed. Every day brings a new uncertainty and can often make us feel like we are parenting on edge. As mothers, we witness our children facing setbacks, anxieties, and insecurities. We worry, too. Is my youngest child thriving? Should I switch schools for my middle schooler, or should we homeschool? Is my son being bullied at football, and if so, what can I do about it? Why does my teenage daughter struggle so much to make quality friendships? Should I allow my tween to have social media? We can analyze and over-analyze and drive ourselves sick. As Dr. Curt Thompson recently said, in the chaos of today's climate, it can feel like we are forced to make crucial parenting decisions while simultaneously driving our vehicle in a snowstorm. Our brains are on high alert and we can easily become overwhelmed. [2] Can you relate?

During her first year of high school, Lilli learned her freshman classes would be virtual and her sports seasons canceled. This was a killer blow. Lil is a stellar athlete and greatly anticipated playing two varsity sports during her rookie high school year. To say she was disappointed when in-person school was canceled was an understatement. This was not easy for her or me, but I was so inspired by Lil's positive outlook and tender spirit. She chose gratitude over grumbling during unprecedented circumstances.

One Saturday, during the months our schools were shut down in Maryland because of COVID-19, I asked my husband to step in to give this Mama a little break. All four of our children had been schooling at home, and I felt exhausted from managing it all. My mothering battery was completely depleted and I was looking forward to a few hours alone to recharge. I wanted to disappear and be "off-duty." Just be by myself. In total silence.

Just as I was about to get out of the door, God again "invited" me to be available to serve Him by caring for my children. A topical skin infection had spread deep into Lilli's foot, which was swollen and in need of expert medical treatment. As I drove Lilli to the hospital, I gripped the wheel and asked our Lord to work through me so I could support my girl on a day when I felt so weary.

At the height of the COVID crisis, we found ourselves in the emergency room. Lord, have mercy. As the ER doctor carefully lanced her foot to give the infection a channel to escape, Lil asked me to hold her hand. Her fingers gripped mine as crocodile tears dripped down her face. The painful process of the doctor exposing her infected wound was brutal but necessary. Lil's foot had to be opened and exposed before it could heal. During that moment, I reflected on how

God had worked through my life since I accepted His calling to have children. It has been the greatest delight of my life and has required me to surrender the most vulnerable places of my heart. Motherhood has sometimes been painful (I hope I didn't scar you too deeply with my vacuum story), but the process of being available for God to use me as a mother has led to deep soul healing and the restoration of my feminine heart.

As we drove away from the hospital, Lilli propped her swollen foot up on the dash, and we sang music at the top of our lungs. Moments later, we came to a dead stop on the freeway because of an accident up ahead, delaying our short trip back home. As we sat there with our vehicle in park, stuck alone together for three hours, Lilli looked over at me and slyly said, "So glad we got to spend some more quality time together, Mom, especially at the hospital." She winked, and I laughed out loud. We turned the music louder and danced in the car. We talked about make-up and social media and her classes. She opened her heart and pursued getting to know mine. That day, when I felt the most ill-equipped to mother and wanted to hide away, has become one of my favorite memories with Lilli.

The mantra in our house after navigating the COVID-19 crisis has been this: hard things produce good things. Mothering these last years has been harder for me, but so much good has come out of it. Mothering right now has been hard, but so much good will *still* come out of it. Do you believe this to be true? Because if you wholeheartedly pursue God's parenting principles, He still has so much good in store for you and your children.

It can be tempting to look at our circumstances, our nation's divisive political climate, natural disasters, cultural tensions, and all of the sickness circulating our world right now and feel like the odds are stacked against us mothers in today's culture. It can feel like our generation of mothers has it harder than any other in history. News pundits tell us we live in a bizarre time; they urge us to find a "new normal." It's easy to feel overwhelmed.

But do you know who else felt this same way? The Christian saints who have lived before us. It's tempting to look at the examples of the men and women whom God "set apart" and feel we have nothing in common. They were holy and out of our league. Perhaps we mistakenly believe God's chosen messengers lived during a much simpler time when their problems were far less complex than the ones we and our children face today. But often the images that are broadcasted of the saints are not as they were.

"We often think of the saints as those so out of touch with the normal struggles of life," said Father Erik Arnold. "We can mistakenly think that somehow they just have no clue about the reality of the struggle that you and I face in daily life. Or, we can figure that if they had struggles in life, that somehow they just walked through it six inches above the ground their whole life. So even if they were around it, they just found it easy to get through it." [3]

In Revelation 7:11, Saint John has a vision of all the saints gathered around the throne of God. Johns saw them worshiping God, saying, "Blessing and glory, wisdom and thanksgiving, honor and power and might be to our God forever and ever." One of the elders spoke up, asking, "Who are these wearing white robes, and where did they come from?" [4] John answers, "These are the ones who have survived the time of great distress."

This is how our Lord describes the saints; they are the ones who survived in their day and age during a time of great distress. The Lord is saying this is who you are meant to be, too. This is what God wants of you, too. The saints aren't the ones who have had it easy. They aren't the ones who have faced zero struggles. They are the ones who have survived the times of great distress. They are survivors. [5]

God was able to use the ones He called as a remarkable testimony of His love. What do we as mothers have in common with the ones God heaped with supernatural courage and grace and summoned to do great things for His kingdom? **We are warriors, too. That is our posture. We are called to rise up and love passionately during these unprecedented times, just like the saints did before us.**

In his reflection on the Saints Father Hans Urs von Balthasar writes, "Those who utter a whole-hearted "Yes" will sometimes stumble, hesitate, or fail to live up to their first ideal, but grace will help them again. They will stick to their path, and very often, it is the case that God's task takes over and relentlessly drags their poor, protesting person ever onward. Thus God has gained the upper hand in them over themselves. It is not they who possess a mission, but their mission possesses them."[6]

This morning, during my quiet hour of prayer, I ask God to use me as a mother to show my children His abundant love. I open my heart up to be His instrument. This afternoon, I grill sourdough sandwiches as I listen to my girls talk about high school. One daughter asks me my opinion on a recent squabble she had with a friend. Another confides that she thinks a boy is cute, but isn't impressed with his character. We eat our warm sandwiches slowly, and then I wipe the counters clean, and our conversations move to college visits and soccer tryouts. We giggle about the last time I took my girls to get their eyebrows waxed (the guy did a hatchet job on my right brow). Lil animatedly tells me a funny story from last week's youth group gathering about a dodgeball gone awry. We unload the dishwasher, and I show her how to prepare dinner in the crockpot. This afternoon at home with my girls feels like such a gift. Slowing our schedule to spend together has given me ample opportunities to shepherd their hearts.

Lilli and I pull on our muck boots and stroll to the backyard to let the chickens out to graze. My little girl is growing into a woman. She is inches taller than me now, just at the age I was when I fell in love with her Daddy. I look at her gliding next to me and smile big. Wasn't it just yesterday, when she was just hours old, and I held her on my chest and tried to imagine what she would be like as a teenager? I had no clue then that she, this blue-eyed girl who made me a mother, would be this...delightful.

We leave the red chicken coop, and our conversation turns to my ministry for mothers. As she tackles high school schooling at home, Lilli has listened patiently to what God has placed on my heart and encouraged me to fight for cracks of time to write. She asks me about the progress of my writing project and how many more hours I think I have until I turn in my manuscript.

"I will never be done, Lilli, until God calls me home! God is constantly teaching me. I am a work in progress," I tell her, and she playfully elbows me.

"I haven't noticed," she teases back. And then she turns to face me, and our eyes lock, and she asks me quietly, "Can I pray for you, Mama, right now? Pray that God will give you what you need to encourage mothers and finish the book God has called you to write?"

I nod yes and choke back the tears as she grabs my hands and petitions God for strength for my writing. We are huddled together in our backyard, her arms sweep around my shoulder, as my girl, who is growing into a young woman, prays for me. And I am blown away by her love. I silently thank God for the life of this soul and that He has trusted me to raise her. It is an honor to shepherd her and see her grow. It is a privilege to be her mother.

I am so grateful I have chosen to lean in and mother where I am most irreplaceable. I want to be all in. I want to be sold out for the Gospel, ministering first at my address. I want to create a haven for my children here at home. A soft place to land where they can come and rest and find shelter from a fallen world. In uncertain times, my home can be a place of security and safety, where they are reminded daily of their true identity. It is well with my soul because Jesus is here. I want to teach my children we have little control over our circumstances, but we can determine our attitude. And we can choose, like the saints before us, to give God glory and praise, even in times of great distress.

When the world seems turned upside down, let's not cower in fear, complaining that we have it tougher as mothers than the generations who have come before us. Let's embrace our call to mother whole-heartedly and let the words of Sr. Carmela of the Holy Spirit be our rallying cry, "We must give every moment its full amount of love, and make each passing moment eternal, by giving it value for eternity." [7] After all, we have a lot of saints to raise for the kingdom of God, and we are all just one breath away from heaven.

23

You Are Irreplaceable And So Abundantly Cherished.

"The loveliest masterpiece of the heart of God is the heart of a mother."
St. Therese of Lisieux

Just last night, around 3 am, our youngest daughter, Annabelle, slipped quietly into our bedroom. Her tiny voice came close to my ear and whispered, "I had a bad dream, and I am scared, Mama. I need you. Can you hold me?" I drew her in and folded her small frame into mine.

"Little one," I whispered in her ear, "You are safe here with me. Do not be afraid of your dreams. You are protected in my arms."

This tiny life rolled over to face me. I could not see her in the dark, but I could feel her heartbeat against my chest and smell her breath on my face. And then she rubbed her nose against mine and said, "Will you tell me about the angels again, Mama? Will you tell me again about how we can trust God and how He promises to protect me?" In that sacred mothering moment, God's Holy Word came flooding back into my memory from my time alone studying the Scriptures, and I whispered to my youngest girl, "Psalm 91:11, "For He will give his angels charge of you to guard you in all of your ways."

187

Just yesterday, Annabelle and I opened the Catechism together to study about angels. She has so many questions at such a tender age, and her heart is like a sponge for spiritual truths. We read how God has given angels a sacred mission, "From its beginning until death, human life is surrounded by their watchful care and intercession. Beside each believer stands an angel as protector and shepherd, leading him to life. We here on earth share our Christian faith in the blessed company of angels, and all men and women united in God." [1]

I felt Annabelle's breathing slow, and her tiny body relax as I whispered prayers of blessing and protection over her. I rubbed her sweet head and she fell peacefully asleep in my arms. And there is no other place I would rather be. An ambassador to this girl. Comfortable in my true identity. Meek. Available. Teachable. I am in awe at how, in parenting this fourth child, God is still parenting me, too.

Last night, the love that pulsated through my soul toward this beautiful girl was intoxicating...intense...supernatural. As I held Annabelle Therese, I felt big, hot tears sting my eyes. Is this how God feels toward me? If so, how much He must love me! For I would give my life for my daughter, and I would do anything in my power to protect her. I cherish her. She delights me. I want what is best for her. I love her, not for what she can do for me or how she makes me feel, but because she was created out of my husband's and my love. And yet, my love is so imperfect. So flawed. So human. But my heavenly Father is perfect love. God is love. He is the Inventor, Sustainer, and Creator of love—my Rescuer. God doesn't choose love. Love is who He is. Unconditional, pure, deep, passionate love. St. Augustine tells us, "God loves each of us as if there was only one of us." [2]

His love for us is faithful and unconditional. It is difficult for us to comprehend the depth of this love, but motherhood gives us a glimpse. Ephesians 3:17-19 tells us, "that Christ may dwell in your hearts through faith; that you, being rooted and grounded in love, may have power to comprehend with all the saints what is the breadth and length and height and depth, and to know the love of Christ which surpasses knowledge, that you may be filled with all the fullness of God."

Before my eyes closed, I paused and thanked God for giving me the privilege of raising four souls, and I prayed to model my posture after His. I smiled that He (for the thousandth time) used motherhood to interrupt my sleep in the middle of the night to remind me just how crazy passionate He is in love with me. And God feels that way about you, too. He is recklessly in awe of you, His beloved daughter. **He will stop at nothing to pursue your heart.**

Motherhood stretches us beyond our limits, past the point where we can no longer rely on ourselves. And thank goodness that's the case because that's where we find Jesus. Our best friend and Savior meets us in the midst of the mess and holds out His gentle hands to cradle our tired ones. Jesus is chasing after a relationship with us. Jesus is chasing after YOU! He invites us daily to "abide" in Him, offering His love to transform and work through our hearts. [3] **How will you choose to live this one sacred life?** "In coming to a decision," writes spiritual director Timothy M. Gallagher, "only one thing is really important— to seek and to find how God is calling me at this time of my life. ... God has created me out of love, and my salvation is found in my living out a return of that love. All my choices, then, must be consistent with this given direction in my life."

My friend, if you have the honor to raise a child (or a crew of them), stay the course. God is inviting you to be His instrument of love. Lean into your divine assignment to shape the souls of your children. Our mother, Mary, gives us the example of her resounding "yes" to God's call to motherhood in extraordinary circumstances. This was her "fiat". It is the Latin word that means "let it be done". Let's look to Mary's acceptance and obedient trust in God's holy invitation to shepherd a soul as our guide. Your "fiat" matters too. You are a soul shaper. Your mothering has eternal value.

Yes, it is true. Hard things produce good things. Take heart, my friend. Be affirmed in your mission of motherhood. God is using you right where you are. Be available. Stand your ground against the arrows of the enemy. Dig into those ordinary moments of motherhood because that is where you have the most influence on your child's heart. The Creator of the world is inviting you to serve as His ambassador. Decide to serve first and best where you matter most. Give your *all* to embracing your sacred calling as a mother. I am rooting for you. You are irreplaceable.

Quo Vadis, Jodi

"Thank you, heroic mothers, for your invincible love!
We thank you for your intrepid trust in God and in His love.
We thank you for the sacrifice of your life."
Saint Pope John Paul II

Take Inventory Of Your Heart

I invite you to pause right now to take inventory of your heart. Reflect on how God is speaking to you today. Consider recording your responses and/ or discuss them with a friend or small group.

1. During this season in your life, where is God inviting you to serve first and best where you matter most? Do you feel like you are holding back part of yourself from your children? Does your heart sometimes feel torn? Jot down some words to describe the struggle you may be feeling. Are you willing to ask God to help you offer your children the parts of your heart you are holding back?

2. Identify a few decisions you have made over the course of the last few months that have caused you to spend less time and energy where you matter most. How did these choices impact your children? What did you learn from them?

3. We have to be careful not to get caught up in doing all of the "things" for our tribe that we miss out on pursuing the chief thing: Motherhood is about shepherding a soul. What often distracts *you* from this main mission? What particular areas of your child's heart have you noticed need "shaping," and how can God use you as His instrument to shepherd that growth?

4. We must remember our true identity does not come from what we do as mothers but from who we are. We need to return daily to the truth of who God says we are. The Holy Scriptures tell us of our true identity. Are you carving out daily time to be in God's Word and to pray? How might you make the principle of saturating yourself in God's love a daily priority, starting today?

5. God has gifted you with distinct passions and gifts. Take a few moments to brainstorm what those might be for you. What comes easiest to you? In what areas are you most complimented? How might God be inviting you to weave your "holy discontent" into your motherhood?

6. Your husband is a gift to you and your children. How do you see the enemy working hard to cause strife in your marriage? How might you do a better job of elevating your husband's role in the family and supporting him? What is one kind thing you can do for him today to remind him you are thankful he is on your parenting team?

7. Enduring hard things often produces good things. List some "hard" things you have encountered as a mother. How have you grown through these challenging situations? What is the toughest thing you are facing right now? Describe what you are learning through these struggles.

8. St. Francis of Assisi said, "Do few things, but do them well; simple joys are holy." What might you need to say no to (for now, not necessarily for always) to be purposeful in ordering your priorities? How can you practically do that?

COMMITMENT TO PRAYER

Consider choosing one from below and committing to praying it every day for one week.

1. Dear Jesus, I ask that this week, you help me serve first and best where I matter the most. Help give me the patience and strength to love my children. Remind me that shaping the souls under my roof is a privilege. Guide me Lord. Amen.

2. Dear God, Thank you so much for assigning _____ to my care. You have given me this particular child on purpose and for your purpose! You, God, have also matched us so that I might grow into a more intimate relationship and reliance on you. Thank you for this opportunity! Give me wisdom on how to mother best. Give me tender arms, a discerning spirit, and a kind voice when I see an area in my child's life that needs shepherding. Amen.

3. Lord, Show me if there is something in my life I prioritize over what you are calling me to do. When I am confused, give me clarity. When I am lonely, be my guide and companion. When I am frustrated, Lord, please help me surrender my will to yours. Jesus, be my steady rock and my greatest advocate. Amen.

4. Lord, I am so worried about _____ and their struggle with _____. I ask that you shoulder this burden. May I have the maturity to give it to you. God, guide me in how to minister to my child. Help me remember that his/her wrestling is not a reflection of me; it is part of his/her story, and you can use it for good. When I am doubting your presence and am

afraid, remind me you are here. When I am tempted to step in and control, nudge me to quiet my heart and trust you. Lord, be with me in this. Capture the heart of my child. Jesus, I need your Sacred Heart. Love through me. Amen.

5. Dear Jesus, How I am weary and overwhelmed by my parenting vocation. Lord, offer me confidence while I mother and please still my worries. I often get caught up in thinking about all of the mistakes I may be making or how my actions could be "ruining" my kids. Remind me that I am human. May I find comfort in the truth that I will make some mistakes. Lord, I boldly ask that You will fill in the gaps when I fall short. Amen.

6. God, Pour your supernatural grace and love into my marriage. Help me to see my husband as you see him. Remind me that he is made in your image and you call him Beloved. God, thank you for giving me the gift of marriage. Please love through me today as I list all of the ways I am grateful for my spouse. Keep the enemy at bay and out of our home. Jesus, fill me up so that I can love with your sacred heart. Amen.

Acknowledgements
To My Crew

This manuscript feels so eerily similar to laboring and birthing a baby. However, unlike my own babies, which stretched and grew my life over a period of nine months, I have been carrying the dream of publishing this work for over a decade. What I learned from this writing and publishing process is that for me, to write is to worship. It is where I am most vulnerable with the Lord, where hours fly by unnoticed in pure bliss, where I relive and testify to the faithfulness and goodness of His love and work in my life. Writing is where my soul sings. Thank you for being my tender audience.

This, my reader, is an offering of my heart. And this is where I pause to acknowledge the significant people who have held my hand along the way, encouraging me to belt out these ballads, to share evidence of God's magnificent work in my life through the gift of motherhood. These friends have encouraged me to worship through this testimony of writing and they are the precious people I want to thank for the remarkable labor of love and delivery of this book. So here goes:

To my BETA readers: Lara Custer, Sonja Minach, Kristy Malik, Amy Caster and Annie Weber. Your detailed feedback and willingness to have the hard conversations about these chapters has been a lifeline to this writer. A big shout-out to Kristy who brainstormed over section titles with me in the final hours before deadlines. You provided so much clarity and encouragement in the final stretch. I will treasure our secret voice texts forever (and pray they self-destruct or else we are big trouble). Thank you sweet friend.

Thank you to Laura White for capturing my delight as I embraced baby Annabelle and for snapping the beautiful picture for this cover. I'm so grateful to Uncle Joe Baranoski for his help with photo editing to make this image usable for the cover. To Beth Patton for early stages of copy editing (you are such a gem!) and Abby McDonald for her honest developmental feedback, professionalism, and genuine encouragement. Thank you to Kati Benton for her copy-editing and for a divine conversation that greatly encouraged me on a day when I needed it most.

Thank you to authors Lisa Brenninkymeyer, Annie Weber, and Laura Phelps for your endorsements. Your ministry work has inspired and molded me. Your mentorship has guided me. Your confidence in my writing has given me permission to share this testimony of love.

To my soul-sisters Charity, Sheila, Shannon, Anne Koch, Bridget, Katie Reedy, Stephanie and Megan Gott. Witnessing your motherhood has been such a gift. You have each ministered to me during critical times when I have wavered in my calling to mother. Thank you for the long walks and sweet teas, your abundant, rich friendship, and for praying for my children. Thank you for accepting desperate phone calls from this Mama when I needed a "witness" to what was happening in my heart. I am grateful for your honesty, sense of humor, and for always seeing the best in my family, even during difficult circumstances.

To Angela, meeting you was a divine appointment and your friendship has been a game changer in my life. Thank you for always pointing me toward the Catholic faith and our Church's wisdom. Thank you for patiently listening to my complaints when I was tired and discouraged and very, very pregnant. (And for always reminding me on my worst days, a handful of chocolate chips makes everything better!) Most of all, thank you for your beautiful heart for motherhood. So many of the principles I write about in this book I have learned from conversations with you. Your friendship has anchored me.

Gratitude to my actual sister-in-laws Brooks, Becky, Christina and Ginny for adopting me as their own sister and for fully embracing my kids. You each bring so much fun and personality to our family. I know you will be there for me and my crew at the drop of a hat to help. We love you so much.

To my spiritual mothers: Sally Proto and Colleen Anderson. Your devotion to your Catholic faith, willingness to listen to my heart, and example of motherhood have shaped who I am today. You have taught me to stay-the-course during difficult seasons of my life and inspired me in the covenant of marriage. I am grateful for your spiritual motherhood.

To my grandmothers: Nanny, you taught me the essence of never shrinking back from hard work. I get my fighting spirit from you. Nana, thank you for your example of a tender heart and your devotion to raising kids as your full time vocation. Even on your deathbed, you mothered extraordinarily well. Grandma Theil, you once sat me down at your little kitchen table and told me that newspaper writing and authorship was a respectable craft and with my skill-set, I should tackle it. Thank you for teaching me to pursue excellence and for your insistence and encouragement to become a writer.

To my Mother-In-Law Debbie Dauses-Smith, thank you for adopting me as a daughter. I am so grateful for your dedication to shaping the heart of my husband and for your example of tenacity and strength in the midst of tremendous loss. You are a heroine. Truly you amaze and inspire me to become better. Thank you for your patient prayers, pointing me toward the Catholic faith, and for your love of the Saints.

To my brothers Jimmy and Bobby. Loving you has been such a delight. Choosing intentionally to live in the same zip-code has been such a joy and helped me grow so much in my walk with Jesus. Thank you for embracing DJ as a brother, for lifting me up, and faithfully cheering on my kids. What a joy to "coach" our tribes alongside each other. You both make me laugh and make me feel so loved. You are two of my closest friends and I cherish you both.

Thank you to my sister Diana. I've been "taken" with you from the moment Mama placed your tiny, beautiful frame into my arms. Thank you for your spirit of vulnerability and for sticking with me through heartbreak, birthing babies, miscarriages, and moves. You love my kids and my husband well. You have listened earnestly to what is stirring my soul, always turning me back to our Lord. You are kind and encouraging, telling me recently, "Stop talking about it Jo and please just write the dang book." (It's finally done Di. Now let's move on to our next topic!) Thank you for blessing our family by marrying Ryan. I'm looking forward to spending forever with you, side by side, in our rocking chairs, under the gaze of Our Heavenly Father. I love you Di. You are my girl, for always. No matter what.

To my nieces and nephews, R.J, Eliza Jane, Skylar, Jessica Lynn, Emma Jo, Maylynn, BoBo, Thea, Jake, Layla, Daisy, Baron, Caroline, Duke, Dolly, Catherine, Jimmy, and Josie. I had no idea I could love you all this much. It makes my head spin. Each of you is fashioned in God's image, yet so unique and special to me. Thank you for embracing me, for opening up your arms to me, for making me feel so abundantly loved. I can not wait to see what God calls each of you to do and how He uses your gifts to tell this world about the hope of His heavenly kingdom. Keep pursuing a relationship with Jesus and just remember - Uncle D.J. and I will be right here cheering you on! Our door is always open and you are most welcome.

To my Dad. My number one cheerleader and the best source of encouragement. The one who always tells me I can do anything I put my mind to. I have so readily received and believed the love of my Heavenly Father because I have had such a fine example of a Father's love from you. You are steady. Patient. Tender. Strong. Knowing how much you treasure me makes me tear up as I write this. I am a Daddy's girl through-and-through. You will always be my first valentine and the first man I loved. (I can't wait for you to book me a segment on national network news to promote this book!) Thank you Papa. I love you.

Thank you to my children Annabelle, Tripp, Lacey, and Lilli. You have captured my heart and this book is just a tiny glimpse of my passionate devotion to you. I pray this work is a reminder of God's abundant love and calling on my life. Mothering you has been my life's greatest privilege. You have gifted me unconditional love, delighted in me, and forgiven me much when I have fallen short. Because of you all, I believe how irreplaceable I am. Dad and I pray, long decades after you each have flown out of our nest to live out your own sacred callings, the six of us will one day spend eternity together sitting at the feet of our Lord, singing praises at the top of our lungs, surrounded by the Saints, angels, and our sweet extended family.

To my mother, if I reach heaven one day, it will be because of you. You introduced me to my Savior Jesus Christ, cultivated a home of tenderness and humility, and set a fire in my soul for God's Word. You have sacrificed much to rear the four of us and taught us so much about friendship and forgiveness. Motherhood has been your greatest work. Thank you for your example. I will always love you. Nothing will change that. Ever. I am honored to be your daughter. You are irreplaceable to me.

Most of all, thank you to my husband D.J. I fell for you from the first moment you asked me to slow-dance during our freshman year at St. Mary's Homecoming Dance. From your gorgeous dimple and blue-eyes, to the way you make me laugh, you've had me from our first "Howdy!" You have never stopped pursuing my heart and have always elevated and honored me. When we were just 16-years-old you told me, "One day I want to marry you because I know you will be an incredible mother and I hope you will have my children." You saw potential in me, before I could see it in myself, encouraging me to joyfully embrace this sacred calling. To give it my all. Your steadfastness and principled heart have anchored me. Our children (and this book) are birthed out of my everlasting love for you. Thank you for choosing me, time and again. I am yours. You have my heart for always. 235.

Citations

INTRODUCTION: THE INLET

*https://www.google.com/books/edition/Inspirational_
Quotes_For_All_Occasions/nXm6BQAAQBAJ
hl=en&gbpv=1&dq=Making+the+decision+to+have+a+child+
is+momentous.++It+is+to+decide+forever+to+have+your+heart+go+
walking+around+outside+of+your+body.+Elizabeth+Stone,+
citation&pg=PT453&printsec=frontcover

PART I: THE PRIVILEGE: EMBRACING YOUR CALLING

THE ASSIGNMENT

[1] "Assignment." Merriam-Webster.com Dictionary, Merriam-Webster, https://www.merriam-webster.com/dictionary/assignment. Accessed 25 Oct. 2020

THE CALLING

[1] LETTER OF HIS HOLINESS POPE FRANCIS TO PRIESTS August 4, 2019. https://www.vatican.va/content/francesco/en/letters/2019/documents/papa-francesco_20190804_lettera-presbiteri.html

[2] https://ifstudies.org/blog/shrinking-american-motherhood-1-in-6-women-in-their-40s-have-never-given-birth- "Shrinking American Motherhood: 1-in-6 Women in Their 40s Have Never Given Birth" November 29, 2022 by Wendy Weng. Accessed Feb 4, 2023

[3] https://www.pewresearch.org/fact-tank/2019/05/08/facts-about-u-s-mothers/ "6 Facts About U.S. Moms" By A.W. Geiger,

Gretchen Livingston, and Kristen Bialik (Pew Research Center) Accessed Feb 5, 2023

[4] https://ifstudies.org/blog/shrinking-american-motherhood-1-in-6-women-in-their-40s-have-never-given-birth- "Shrinking American Motherhood: 1-in-6 Women in Their 40s Have Never Given Birth" November 29, 2022 by Wendy Weng. Accessed Feb 4, 2023

[5] https://www.pewresearch.org/fact-tank/2019/05/08/facts-about-u-s-mothers/ "6 Facts About U.S. Moms" By A.W. Geiger, Gretchen Livingston, and Kristen Bialik (Pew Research Center) Accessed Feb 5, 2023

[6] Gress, Carrie. *The Anti-Mary Exposed: Rescuing the Culture From Toxic Femininity* TAN Books Charlotte, North Carolina 2019 pg. 12.

[7] Gress, Carrie. *The Anti-Mary Exposed: Rescuing the Culture From Toxic Femininity* TAN Books Charlotte, North Carolina 2019 pg. 13.

[8] Ciraulo, Allison. https://churchlifejournal.nd.edu/articles/motherhood-as-a-path-to-sainthood/ *Motherhood as a Path to Sainthood* October 10, 2016. Accessed April 17, 2023

[9] Pierlot, Holly. *A Mother's Rule of Life (How to bring order to your home and peace to your soul)* Sophia Institute Press, 2014 Pg. 108

[10] https://en.wikiquote.org/wiki/C._S._Lewis, accessed October 9, 2023

[11] Clarkson, Sally. Mission of Motherhood: Touching Your Child's Heart For Eternity, WaterBrook; 1st Edition (January 21, 2003), 43.

[12] (No. 16, *Letter to Families*) 1994 - YEAR OF THE FAMILY, Letter to Families from Pope John Paul II, Gratissimam Sane

[13] https://www.usccb.org/beliefs-and-teachings/how-we-teach/catechesis/catechetical-sunday/prayer/theological-reflection-hater *Embracing Our Universal Call to Holiness* by Rev. Robert J. Hater, PhD. Accessed May 5, 2023

[14] Second Vatican Council, (*Lumen Gentium, 39*).

[15] Pope Francis

MESSAGE OF HIS HOLINESS POPE FRANCIS FOR THE 56th WORLD DAY OF VOCATIONS 2019 The courage to take a risk for God's promise

https://www.vatican.va/content/francesco/en/messages/vocations/documents/papa-francesco_20190131_56-messaggio-giornata-mondiale-vocazioni.html

[16] Peter Kreeft, *Jesus Shock*, St. Augustines Press; 1st Edition (April 30, 2020), 57.

IGNITING A DESIRE

*https://cardinalwinningprolifeinitiative.wordpress.com/2012/10/25/the-godliness-of-motherhood/

[1] L. B. Cowman and James Reimann, *Streams In The Desert: 366 Daily Devotional Readings.* First published in 1925. Zondervan; Revised Edition (June 1, 1999). Entry excerpt by Frederick William Roberston, 312.

[2] Colleen C. Mitchell, *Who Does He Say You Are? Women Transformed by Christ in the Gospels*, Franciscan Media (August 5, 2016), 3.

[3] Ibid.

[4] Ruth Schwenk, *The Better Mom: Growing in Grace between Perfection and the Mess,* Zondervan (April 24, 2018), 18-19.

[5] L. B. Cowman and James Reimann, *Streams In The Desert: 366 Daily Devotional Readings.* First published in 1925. Zondervan; Revised Edition (June 1, 1999). Entry excerpt by Frederick William Roberston, 313.

A PRIESTLY REVELATION FOR MOTHERHOOD

* https://bigccatholics.blogspot.com/2017/01/pope-benedict-xvi-on-prayer.html

[1] Father Jacques Philippe, *Searching for and Maintaining Peace: A Small Treatise On Peace Of Heart,* Alba House; 1St Edition (January 18, 2002), page 6

A DIVINE PRIVILEGE

*https://www.taylor-mademama.com/career-mom-to-stay-at-home-mom-how-to-find-confidence-in-the-way-you-do-mom-life/children-are-not-a-distraction-from-more-important-work-they-are-the-most-important-work-c-s-lewis/

[1] https://www.researchgate.net/publication/8479969_Breastfeeding_Maintaining_an_irreplaceable_immunological_resource *Breastfeeding: Maintaining an irreplaceable immunological resource* Authors Miriam Labbok, David Clark, Armond S Goldman. Accessed May 18, 2023

[2] B*reastfeeding can be the difference between life and deat*h - World Food Program (WFP) 1 August 2017, Lauren Landis

https://www.wfp.org/stories/breastfeeding-can-be-difference-between-life-and-death Accessed May 19, 2023

[3] *BREASTFEEDING PROVIDES IRREPLACEABLE BENEFITS FOR BABIES*

PUBLISHED ON AUG 18, 2020

https://www.pasadenanow.com/weekendr/breastfeeding-provides-irreplaceable-benefits-for-babies/ Dr. Liz Diaz-Querol with Kaiser Permanente Southern California.

The Pasadena Now WeekendR. Accessed May 19, 2023

[4] Ibid. https://www.pasadenanow.com/weekendr/breastfeeding-provides-irreplaceable-benefits-for-babies/

[5] Sally Clarkson, Mission of Motherhood: Touching Your Child's Heart For Eternity, WaterBrook; 1st Edition (January 21, 2003), 63.

A DIVIDED HEART

[1] https://www.goodreads.com/quotes/571133-to-the-world-you-may-be-one-person-but-to, Accessed October 24, 2023

[2] *Ignatius Catholic Study Bible New Testament* Ignatius Press, San Francisco 2010

(With Introduction, Commentary, and Notes by Scott Hahn and Curtis Mitch), pg 18.

SERVING FIRST WHERE I AM MOST IRREPLACEABLE

[1] Https://www.desiringgod/org/articles/do-the-next-thing, Accessed October 23, 2023

[2] Conversation with Barbara Curano, licensed Catholic therapist. (Need to confirm date)

[3] Ibid.

[4] Clarkson, Sally. Mission of Motherhood: Touching Your Child's Heart For Eternity, WaterBrook; 1st Edition (January 21, 2003), 53.

THE ASSIGNMENT DESK

[1] Clarkson, Sally. Mission of Motherhood: Touching Your Child's Heart For Eternity, WaterBrook; 1st Edition (January 21, 2003), 43-44.

[2] Pope Paul IV, *Of Human Life (Humane Vitae)*, Pauline Books & Media; Annotated edition (August 23, 2018), #10.

[3] Gaudium et Spes: On The Church In The Modern World (Vatican Council II) #48

[4] Gaudium et Spes: On The Church In The Modern World (Vatican Council II) #50

[5] Dr. Scott Hahn, Contraception is contrary to God's law: Why the Hahns became Roman Catholic. Posted on 10/5/2012, 6:22:55 AM by koinonia http://www.freerepublic.com/focus/f-religion/2940510/posts

[6] Danielle Bean, Momnipotent: The Not-So-Perfect Woman's Guide to Catholic Motherhood Ascension Press (April 8, 2014), 11. move

[7] Katrina J. Zeno, Discovering The Feminine Genius: Every Women's Journey (Boston Pauline Books and Media, 2010), 41.

YOU BLINDED ME WITH SCIENCE

[1] Carrie Gress, *The Anti-Mary Exposed: Rescuing the Culture From Toxic Femininity,* 18, 19.

[2] Erica Komisar *Being There: Why Prioritizing Motherhood in the First Three Years Matters,* Hardcover Publisher : TarcherPerigee (April 11, 2017) xii, Introduction

[3] Ibid. pg. 4

[4] (Jim Dryden, "Nurturing during Preschool Years Boosts Child's Brain Growth," Washington University School of Medicine, St. Louis, April 25, 2016, medicine.wust.edu/news/nurturing-preschool-years-boosts-childs-brain-growth.)

[5] (Stanford University of Medical Center, "Mom's Voice Activates Many Different Regions in Children's Brains, Study Shows," *Science Daily,* May 16, 2016, sciencedaily.com/ releases/2016/05/160516181017.htm.

[6] Carrie Gress, *The Anti-Mary Exposed: Rescuing the Culture From Toxic Femininity,* 12, 13.

[7] Kate O'Beirne, *Women Who Make the World Worse* (New York: Sentinel, 2006), xxii.

[8] Erica Komisar *Being There: Why Prioritizing Motherhood in the First Three Years Matters,* Hardcover Publisher : TarcherPerigee (April 11, 2017)(xii)

[9] Ibid (xv)

[10] Ibid (xiv)

[11] Ibid. (xiii)

[12] James Tooley, *The Miseducation of Women* (Chicago: Ivan R, 2003), 192.

[13] Erica Komisar *Being There: Why Prioritizing Motherhood in the First Three Years Matters,* Hardcover Publisher : TarcherPerigee (April 11, 2017), 3.

PART II : THE PRINCIPLES: LIVING OUT YOUR CALLING

THE AMBASSADOR

[1] https://www.merriam-webster.com/dictionary/ambassador, Accessed October 24, 2023

[2] Paul David Tripp, *Parenting: 14 Gospel Principles That Can Radically Change Your Family*, Crossway; 1st edition (September 30, 2016), 14.

[3] Ibid., 20.

[4] Peter Kreeft, *Jesus Shock* Wellspring (June 11, 2012), 146.

[5] Ginger Hubbard, *Don't Make Me Count To Three,* Shepherd Press; 39577th edition (March 1, 2004), 22.

AVAILABLE

[1] https://www.merriam-webster.com/dictionary/available, Accessed October 11, 2019

[2] "Laura Phelps :You Are Not Enough, " *Walking With Purpose* (blog), September 22, 2020, https://walkingwithpurpose. com/you-are-not-enough/?utm_medium=email&utm_ campaign=Weekly%20Walking%20With%20 Purpose&utm_content=Weekly%20Walking%20With%20 Purpose+CID_eb66f725dc13e3edc1e785326c345932&utm_ source=CM&utm_term=You%20Are%20Not%20Enough

[3] Dr. Meg Meeker, *The 10 Habits of Happy Mothers: Reclaiming Our Passion, Purpose, and Sanity,* Ballantine Books; 1st edition (September 6, 2011).

[4] "Venerable Margherita "Margaret" Occhiena", Salesian Missions, October 26, 2020, https://salesianmissions.org/about-us/who-we-are/about-st-john-bosco/our-history/history-of-the-salesians/ venerable-margaret-occhiena/

[5] "Holy Moms: Four Saints Who Were Mothers", October 25, 2020, https://catholic-link.org/images/infographic-holy-moms-saints-mothers/

[6] "Venerable Margherita "Margaret" Occhiena", Salesian Missions, October 26, 2020, https://salesianmissions.org/about-us/who-we-are/about-st-john-bosco/our-history/history-of-the-salesians/venerable-margaret-occhiena/

[7] Sally Clarkson, *The Mission of Motherhood: Touching Your Child's Heart For Eternity,* WaterBrook; 1st edition (January 21, 2003), 63.

[8] https://bookroo.com/quotes/elisabeth-elliot, Accessed October 24, 2023

AUDIENCE OF ONE

*https://www.ccel.org/ccel/desales/love.all.html, Accessed October 24, 2023

[1] Philip Yancey *"Our Daily Bread"* https://odb.org/2008/08/27/an-audience-of-one/.

[2] https://churchlifejournal.nd.edu/articles/motherhood-as-a-path-to-sainthood/

Motherhood as a Path to Sainthood by Allison Ciraulo October 10, 2016, accessed April 17, 2023

[3] https://summitlife.org/an-audience-of-one-summitlife-today-september-14-2015/

[4] Amy R. Buckley *"In the Midst of the Mess: Hagar and the God Who Sees."* https://www.cbeinternational.org/resources/article/mutuality/midst-mess-hagar-and-god-who-sees

UNDERSTANDING YOUR VALUE: YOU ARE WORTH MORE THAN YOU THINK

*Carrie Gress, *The Anti-Mary Exposed: Rescuing the Culture From Toxic Femininity,* 12, 13. (Confirm page #)

[1] Lisa Brenninkmeyer Walking With Purpose "Seven Priorities That Make Life Work"

Beacon Publishing, 2013. The Dynamic Catholic Institute, Hebron KY. Pg 78

[2] pg. 79

[3] Lisa Brenninkmeyer Ordering Your Priorities "Building a Life Well Lived"

Walking With Purpose Inc. pg 17

[4] https://churchlifejournal.nd.edu/articles/motherhood-as-a-path-to-sainthood/

Motherhood as a Path to Sainthood by Allison Ciraulo October 10, 2016, accessed April 17, 2023

[5] (Pg 106) Holly

[6] pg. 146 A Mother's Rule of Life (Holly Pierlot)

[7] Pg 108

[8] Lisa Brenninkmeyer Walking With Purpose "Seven Priorities That Make Life Work"

Beacon Publishing, 2013. The Dynamic Catholic Institute, Hebron KY. Pg 79

[9] https://www.mother.ly/parenting/sahms-would-earn-162k-survey-finds/

"If SAHMs were paid, their salary would be $184K/year" By Emily Glover Updated February 22, 2023 (According to 2021 available data from salary.com)

[10] Sarah Reynolds, Vice President of Marketing at Salary.com. https://www.salary.com/articles/mother-salary/ How Much Is a Mother Really Worth? Accessed 4/28/23 salary.com

[11] https://www.washingtonpost.com/news/monkey-cage/wp/2018/08/23/most-americans-vastly-underestimate-how-rich-they-are-compared-with-the-rest-of-the-world-does-it-matter/ accessed 04/25/23

[12] The Catechism of the Catholic Church, Publisher: Bantam Doubleday Dell, #1666

[13] Ibid.

[14] Allison Ciraulo

https://churchlifejournal.nd.edu/articles/motherhood-as-a-path-to-sainthood/

Motherhood as a Path to Sainthood by Allison Ciraulo October 10, 2016, accessed April 17, 2023

[15] Celine Martin, Sister Genevieve of the Holy Face *"The Mother of the Little Flower"*. *Pg. 9*

[16] Ibid. pg 18

[17] Ibid. pg 18, Letter of June 25, 1877

[18] Ibid. (Letter of September 7, 1877?) pg. 19

[19] Ibid. Pg. 20

SOUL SHAPER

*https://www.takeupandread.org/community/2021/8/3/call-me-blessed-esther, Accessed October 24, 2023

[1] Ginger Hubbard, *Don't Make Me Count To Three* (Shepherd Press: March 1, 2004), 21.

[2] *Matthew 16:25-26; John 15:13, Acts 2:41.*

[3] *The Catechism of the Catholic Church*, Publisher: Bantam Doubleday Dell, *#363*

[4] *Ibid., #366*

[5] Ginger Hubbard, *Don't Make Me Count To Three* (Shepherd Press: March 1, 2004), 22.

[6] ouis M. Notkin, ed, *Mother Tributes from the World's Greatest Literature* (New York: Samuel Curl, 1943), 177.

[7] Mabel Bartlett and Sophia Baker, *Mothers- Makers of Men* (New York: Expositions Press, 1952), 92.

[8] *The Catechism of the Catholic Church*, Publisher: Bantam Doubleday Dell, #355

[9] Ibid, #356

[10] Ibid, #357

[11] Luigi Giussani, *The Risk of Education: Discovering Our Ultimate Destiny* (New York: Crossroad Publishing, 1995)

[12] *Catechism of the Catholic Church, 2nd edition* (Vatican: Libreria Editrice Vaticana, 2012), Prayer as Covenant. #2563, 614.

[13] Lisa Brenninkmeyer, *Ordering Your Priorities: Building a Life Well Lived* (Printed in The United States of America, Walking With Purpose Inc., 2021), 147.

[14] Pope Francis, *Joy of the Gospel* (Erlanger, KY: Dynamic Catholic Institute, 2014), 97.

[15] *Catechism of the Catholic Church, 2nd edition* (Vatican: Libreria Editrice Vaticana, 2012), Prayer as God's Gift. #2560, 614.

[16] Clarkson, Sally. *Mission of Motherhood: Touching Your Child's Heart For Eternity,* WaterBrook; 1st Edition (January 21, 2003), 43.

DELIGHT IN ME

*https://media.benedictine.edu/5-things-st-ignatius-taught-me-about-myself, Accessed October 20, 2023

[1] ttp://www.therealpresence.org/archives/Saints/Saints_027.htm.
Devotion of St. Thérèse of Lisieux to the Blessed Virgin Mary by Fr. John A. Hardon, S.J. Vol. 11, March 1952, pp. 75-84. Accessed July 20, 2023

[2] St. Teresa of Avila, *Interior Castle*, trans. Allison Peers (New York: Doubleday, 1989), 38.

[3] Janet P. Penley with Diane Eble, *Motherstyles: using personality type to discover your parenting strengths, (*1st Da Capo Press ed. 2006), 3.

[4] Ibid.

[5] Max Lucado, *Cure for the Common Life Small Group Study,* (Thomas Nelson: September 19, 2006), v.

[6] *Ignatius Study Bible: New Testament*, Ignatius Press (June 1, 2010), 1 Corinthians 12:4-6

[7] Art and Laraine Bennett, *The Temperament God Gave You: The Classic Key to Knowing Yourself, Getting Along with Others, and Growing Closer to the Lord,* (Sophia Institute Press: June 15, 2005),13.

[8] Ibid., page 13

[9] Ibid., page 18

[10] Ibid., page 1

Confirm this is cut!

[8] Ibid., page 11

PART III: THE POSTURE: PROTECTING YOUR CALLING

YOU'D BETTER BELIEVE…YOU ARE UNDER ATTACK!

[1] Fr. John Riccardo, *Unshakeable Hope In The Midst Of The Storm.* The Word Amount Us Press. August 26, 2023. https://www.amazon.com/Unshakeable-Hope-Midst-Storm-Riccardo/dp/1593257155

[2] John Riccardo, *Heaven Starts Now: Becoming a Saint Day by Day*

THE ATTITUDE

[1] https://walkingwithpurpose.com/getting-naked-in-the-garden/ Jodi Dauses, "Getting Naked In The Garden", Walking With Purpose Blog. Published July 28, 2020

[2] https://www.todayintheword.org/daily-devotional/pray-for-one-another

[3] James Clear, *Atomic Habits* An Easy & Proven Way to Build Good Habits & Break Bad Ones , Avery Publishing, Hardcover – October 16, 2018 (need page number)

THE WAR ZONE

*https://annvoskamp.com/2021/05/get-what-you-really-want-for-mothers-day-and-get-what-you-really-need-to-know-about-mothering/

[1] *The Catechism of the Catholic Church*, Publisher: Bantam Doubleday Dell, #368 and Jeremiah 31:33

[2] Ted Tripp, *Shepherding A Child's Heart*, Shepherd Press (January 1, 1995), 4

SLEEPING WITH THE ENEMY

*https://www.orthodoxchurchquotes.com/category/sayings-from-saints-elders-and-fathers/st-john-chrysostom/ Accessed December 5, 2023.

St. John Chrysostom, Homily 20, Homilies on Galatians, Ephesians, Philippians, Colossians, Thessalonians, Timothy, Titus, and Philemon

[1] Father John Bartunek. "How Can I Identify My Root Sin?" https://spiritualdirection.com/2010/04/26/how-can-i-identify-my-root-sin

[2] Ibid.

[3] Ibid.

[4] Claire Dwyer, "Humility and High Ideals" Part 37 of This Present Paradise, A Series of Reflections on St. Elizabeth of the Trinity, September 17, 2020, (https://spiritualdirection.com/2020/09/17/humility-and-high-ideals.

[5] Ibid.

[6] Ibid.

IGNORING WHAT STIRS OUR HEARTS

https://www.catholicnewsagency.com/resource/245726/pope-francis-in-colombia-encounter-with-clergy, Accessed January 3, 2023

[1] Bill Hybels, *Holy Discontent: Feuling the Fire That Ignites Personal Vision,* Zondervan (May 27, 2007), 25.

[2] Ibid.

[3] Ibid., 26.

[4] Ibid.

[5] Lisa Brenninkmeyer, Walking With Purpose: Seven Priorities That Make Life Work, Wellspring (April 23, 2013), 172.

[6] Bill Hybels, Holy Discontent: Feuling the Fire That Ignites Personal Vision, Zondervan (May 27, 2007), 27.

[7] Lisa Brenninkmeyer, Walking With Purpose: Seven Priorities That Make Life Work, Wellspring (April 23, 2013), 172.

IRREPLACEABLE, NOT INEXHAUSTIBLE

[1] J.D. Salinger, Catcher in The Rye, Published January 30th 2001 by Back Bay Books (first published July 16th 1951) New York City, New York,1949 (United States) Agerstown, Pennsylvania,1949 (United States), pg 32. ISBN 0316769177 (ISBN13: 9780316769174)

[2] Bill Hybels, Simplify: Ten Practices To Unclutter Your Soul. Tyndale Momentum; Reprint edition (May 1, 2015), 6.

[3] Ibid., 6, 7.

[4] Ibid., 12,

[5] Ibid.

[6] https://diocesan.com/a-martyr-for-the-anxious/, Accessed March 20, 2023

[7] Priscilla Shirer, Awaken: 90 Days With The God Who Speaks. B&H Books (August 15, 2017), 4.

[8] Ibid.

[9] Priscilla Shirer, Awaken: 90 Days With The God Who Speaks. B&H Books (August 15, 2017), 4.

[10] Saint Faustina Divine Mercy of The Soul (2; 921) *need to confirm page #

[11] Dr. Richard A. Swenson, Margin: Restoring Emotional, Physical, Financial, and Time Reserves to Overloaded Lives. NavPress; 1st edition (October 25, 2004), 13.

[12] Ibid.

[13] Lisa Terkerust, *The Best Yes: Making Wise Decisions in the Midst of Endless Demands* Thomas Nelson (August 19, 2014), 236.

[14] Ibid., 64.

[15] Ibid., 171.

[16] Priscilla Shirer, *The Resolution for Women,* B&H Books; Original edition (September 1, 2011), 91.

[17] Ibid.

[18] Lisa Terkerust, *The Best Yes: Making Wise Decisions in the Midst of Endless Demands* Thomas Nelson (August 19, 2014), 249.

FORGET YOUR PRIMARY MISSION FIELD? CHECK YOUR DRIVER'S LICENSE

[1] Clarkson, Sally. *The Mission of Motherhood,* pg. 44

[2] Allison Ciraulo. *Motherhood as a Path to Sainthood*

https://churchlifejournal.nd.edu/articles/motherhood-as-a-path-to-sainthood/

Motherhood as a Path to Sainthood by Allison Ciraulo October 10, 2016. Accessed April 17, 2023

[3] Paul David Tripp, Parenting: 14 Gospel Principles That Can Radically Change Your Family, Crossway; 1st edition (September 30, 2016), 76.

[4] Ibid., 75.

PARENTING DURING UNPRECEDENTED TIMES

[1] Homily by Father Erik Arnold, Times of Great Distress, https://boxcast.tv/highlights/sunday-mass-on-november-1-2020-640281/lfgv28pq8k6lau0auexn/zhkq5wpparmispitqkt6?fbclid=IwAR3uozESiP6us9rnW_iS-O1g5dH8I6KPH_k3wkRIb0HE-0prl4OEVE-LfWw, accessed November 1, 2020.

[2] Allen, Jennie, "02-Shame is more common than you think with Dr. Curt Thompson. " *Made For This,* season 6, episode 02, 30 September 2020.

[3] Homily by Father Erik Arnold, *Times of Great Distress,* https://boxcast.tv/highlights/sunday-mass-on-november-1-2020-640281/lfgv28pq8k6lau0auexn/zhkq5wpparmispitqkt6?fbclid=IwAR3uozESiP6us9rnW_iS-O1g5dH8I6KPH_k3wkRIb0HE-0prl4OEVE-LfWw, accessed November 1, 2020.

[4] Revelation 7:13, Saint Joseph Edition of the New American Bible, Catholic Book Publishing Co. New York (July 27, 1970).

[5] Homily by Father Erik Arnold, *Times of Great Distress,* https://boxcast.tv/highlights/sunday-mass-on-november-1-2020-640281/lfgv28pq8k6lau0auexn/zhkq5wpparmispitqkt6?fbclid=IwAR3uozESiP6us9rnW_iS-O1g5dH8I6KPH_k3wkRIb0HE-0prl4OEVE-LfWw, accessed November 1, 2020.

[6] Hans Urs von Balthasar, *You Crown the Year With Your Goodness.* Ignatius Press; First edition (November 1, 1989), 205.

[7] Father Gabriel of St. Mary Magdalen, O.C.D. Divine Intimacy: Meditations on the Interior Life For Every Day Of The Liturgical Year, Baronius Press (Sr. Carmela of the Holy Spirit, O.C.D,) pg. 101

YOU ARE IRREPLACEABLE AND SO ABUNDANTLY CHERISHED.

[1] St. Augustine, https://www.catholicdigest.com/from-the-magazine/quiet-moment/st-augustine-god-loves-each-of-us/, Accessed December 1, 2023.

[2] *The Catechism of the Catholic Church*, Publisher: Bantam Doubleday Dell, # 336.

[3] John 15:5, *Saint Joseph Edition of the New American Bible*, Catholic Book Publishing Co. New York (July 27, 1970).

[1] https://aleteia.org/2022/07/12/st-john-paul-iis-powerful-words-to-all-heroic-mothers-for-choosing-life/ St. John Paul II's powerful words to all "heroic mothers" for choosing life, published 7/12/22 by Philip Kosloski. Aleteia. Accessed December 5, 2023

REFLECTION QUESTIONS: TAKE INVENTORY OF YOUR HEART

[1] Ginger Hubbard, *Don't Make Me Count To Three,* (Shepherd Press: March 1, 2004), 21.